PRICED

OUT

PRICED

OUT

*The Economic and Ethical Costs
of American Health Care*

Uwe E. Reinhardt

Forewords by Paul Krugman
and Sen. William H. Frist

PRINCETON UNIVERSITY PRESS

Princeton and Oxford

Requests for permission to reproduce material from this work
should be sent to permissions@press.princeton.edu

Published by Princeton University Press
41 William Street, Princeton, New Jersey 08540
6 Oxford Street, Woodstock, Oxfordshire OX20 1TR

press.princeton.edu

Library of Congress Control Number: 2019932481
ISBN 978-0-691-19217-8

British Library Cataloging-in-Publication Data is available

Editorial: Joe Jackson and Jacqueline Delaney
Production Editorial: Karen Carter
Text and Jacket Design: Pam Schnitter
Production: Erin Suydam
Publicity: Julia Hall and James Schneider
Copyeditor: Barbara Goodhouse

Jacket image of author, courtesy of Princeton University

This book has been composed in Garamond Pro and Filosofia

Printed on acid-free paper. ∞

Printed in the United States of America

1 3 5 7 9 10 8 6 4 2

I would like to thank Tsung-Mei Cheng, Health Policy Research Analyst, Woodrow Wilson School of Public and International Affairs, Princeton University, for her many contributions to this book.

CONTENTS

FOREWORD

Paul Krugman

When Uwe Reinhardt died in 2017, many people, myself included, lost a friend; the world at large lost one of its leading experts on the economics of health care. But Uwe was a moral as well as an intellectual force.

Uwe's professional reputation rested to a large extent on his brilliant analyses of the forces driving health care costs. In particular, he did more than anyone to document and elucidate the inefficiency and sheer craziness of the U.S. health system. His most famous paper (with Gerald Anderson, Peter Hussey, and Varduhi Petrosyan) was titled "It's the Prices, Stupid: Why the United States Is So Different from Other Countries." It showed that while America spends much more than any other country on health care, it doesn't actually get more care—it just pays higher prices.

Nor was he merely an analyst and a critic. Although he never mentions it in his book, Uwe, together with his colleague and wife, Tsung-Mei Cheng, helped devise Taiwan's highly successful single-payer health care system, which is both an object lesson in how to avoid the worst of the pathologies we experience here and a demonstration of how we could do far better.

But Uwe Reinhardt was much more than a clinician, diagnosing the ills of insurers and hospitals and prescribing treatment. For he never forgot the forest for the trees. He never lost sight of the purpose of our, or anyone's, health care system: to prevent illness where possible, to treat it where necessary. And he never forgot that the fundamental flaw in the U.S. system wasn't technical; it was its failure to serve that higher purpose. It was always obvious to those who knew him, and I suspect to his readers as well, that behind the incisiveness of his analysis and the wit of his commentary—for Uwe was a very, very funny man—lay a fine sense of outrage at the way the sacred task of medicine has been corrupted by cruelty and greed.

Priced Out: The Economic and Ethical Costs of American Health Care is, alas, Uwe's final book. Fittingly, as the title suggests, it's a book that showcases both sides of his professional persona.

The first half of the book is a brisk but fact-filled tour through what he calls the "wonderland" of U.S. health care. That's not a term of praise: the wondrous thing is how bad a system we've managed to build.

For anyone coming at this subject fresh, the book's tour of the system will come as a revelation, and not in a good way. Even people who have paid considerable attention to health care issues will be richly rewarded—which is to say, disgusted—by the details of dysfunctionality he documents, by the overpayment and bloat that make U.S. health care as expensive as it is.

For example, although I'm not a health economist—I just play one on TV, sometimes—I've written about health economics for many years (with Uwe giving me crucial guidance and helping me avoid big mistakes). Yet I didn't know the extent to which administrators, not caregivers, now dominate the health care workforce. According to Robert Kocher, MD, of Venrock Capital, "Today, for every doctor, only 6 of the 16 non-doctor workers have clinical roles." The other ten are administrative and management staff, most of whom aren't helping to provide care, even indirectly.

Nor did I fully appreciate just how wildly variable the costs of any given medical procedure are, even in the same city (indeed, the same hospital), and how invisible this variation of costs is to patients.

There's an influential school of policy thought that advocates "consumer-based" health care, that is, trying to make shopping for health care more like shopping for cars or cell phones. Members of this school argue that we can save money by giving patients "skin in the game," that is, making them pay a larger share of costs out of pocket. As Uwe points out, the available evidence says that this doesn't actually work—and anyone trying to understand why should read his description of what really faces patients, who don't know either the value of treatment or how much anything will cost them. They are, as he says, "like blindfolded shoppers pushed into a department store to shop around smartly."

What emerges from all of this is a devastating portrait of a system that doesn't just consume huge resources to no good end, but denies care to many Americans, not because it would really be too expensive to provide, but because the system prices them out by making care arbitrarily expensive—and/or rations health care in ways that are fundamentally indefensible.

For that is the theme both of the book's prologue, which highlights the ethical issues at the core of health care, and the whole second half, which shows how our collective refusal to face up to ethical choices has led to a system that's both cruel and inefficient.

As Uwe says, the crucial question is one that he stated in a *Journal of the American Medical Association* article after the failure of the 1993 Clinton health plan: Should a child of a poor American family have the same chance of receiving adequate prevention and treatment as the child of a rich family?

Libertarians would argue that the principles of economic freedom prohibit government intervention to force equality in health care, no matter how unfair the outcomes may seem. That's a defensible philosophical position. But few are willing to take that position openly. Instead, Uwe found himself attacked as a "socialist propagandist" for even asking the question.

The reason, as *Priced Out* makes clear at some length, is that many people in our political system want to have it both ways. What they really favor and are trying to impose is a system in which health care is "rationed by income class," with only the well-off receiving the full benefits of modern medicine. But saying that openly would be very unpopular, so they never admit their real goals, instead pretending that their policies would be good for everyone. And they lash out with accusations of "socialism," not to mention personal attacks on anyone who tries to get at the real issue.

And as Uwe points out, even those on the other side of the U.S. political spectrum, who basically—like the citizens of every other advanced country—say yes to the Reinhardt question, are afraid to say so forthrightly, perhaps because they're afraid of being labeled as socialists. "Americans," he writes, "typically shy away from an explicit statement on social ethics in debating health reform. Instead, that debate is couched mainly in terms of technical parameters."

Now, *Priced Out* goes on to provide a spectacularly lucid guide to the way those technical parameters, from community rating to the structure of subsidies, determine the way health care proposals affect ordinary families. If you want the best explanation I've seen of what community rating is, why you need it to make health care available to people with high medical risks, and why it's not enough by itself—why you need a structure that looks like Obamacare—*Priced Out* has it.

Uwe also does a fine job of skewering the shibboleths that still distort our discussions of alternatives to the current U.S. system. To those who say that single-payer is un-American, something the U.S. public would never accept, he points out that every American over sixty-five already lives under a single-payer system—for that's what Medicare is. To those who complain about the cost of the subsidies that made the expansion of coverage under the Affordable Care Act (ACA, a.k.a. Obamacare) possible, he points out that the hidden subsidies the tax code gives to employment-based insurance, by making health benefits nontaxable, are about three times the $100 billion a year we spend to subsidize coverage under the ACA.

But he's right: you can't even begin to discuss the virtues and vices of policy proposals, from Obamacare to Republican alternatives to the new push for single-payer, unless you first get your ethical principles straight. Is your goal to make sure that everyone has comparable access to health care or not? If it isn't—and Republicans make it clear by their actions that for them, it isn't—you should say so.

If you think it's unusual to see a consummate expert in the details of health care chastise people for focusing too much, too soon, on the technical aspects rather than on the ethics, you're right. But Uwe Reinhardt was an unusual economist—and a superior human being.

As I said, Uwe was a very funny guy, and his humor shines through *Priced Out*—but so does his moral seriousness. He wanted us to understand the nuts and bolts of how health care systems work. In particular, he wanted us to understand the U.S. system's many loose screws. But he also wanted us to treat decisions about how to manage health economics as fundamentally ethical questions—indeed, matters of life and death. Because that's what health care is all about.

FOREWORD

Senator William H. Frist, MD

I learned a lot from Uwe Reinhardt over forty-eight years. He is, as the reader will uncover in the pages ahead, the master teacher.

My first real exposure to much of the content of this book was as an undergraduate in the early 1970s. Yes, as Uwe so fondly recalled in our many subsequent speeches together, I was one of the "Reinhardt groupies" who immediately after every lecture would traipse to the front of the old lecture hall, gather around the energized young professor with the German accent, and pepper him with questions. The sparring and banter were magical. An hour later we would depart our mosh pit, much wiser, but more importantly, more excited and curious about learning than ever—all to be repeated at the next lecture.

It's way too easy to idealize a lifelong teacher and mentor, but it is not an exaggeration to say he changed me and transformed my worldview for the better. I have known him as no one else has.

We were together side by side in the hospital operating room as I conducted my very last heart transplant before entering the Senate. Eager to experience firsthand the realities of what he was teaching, he flew through the night in a small twin-engine plane with me, dressed in green scrubs, with a red Igloo cooler containing the donor human heart I had just removed resting against his leg on the bumpy flight.

We were together when he testified before the health committee (as he frequently was called upon to do) I was chairing in the Senate, jokingly opening his always enlightening testimony, verbally painting an image of me as a curious, shabbily dressed freshman at Princeton.

We were together in South Africa, jointly lecturing on behavioral economics (with a side trip to the World Cup, where he knew the bio and record of every single player on both teams).

We were together when he and his wife May double-dated at the world-famous songwriter haven Bluebird Café in Nashville on my first date with my wife, Tracy. (He knew the words to every country song, to the amusement of each songwriter.)

And we were together in 2007 at Princeton, the year after I had left the Senate, when, almost as if in a chapter in a storybook, I had the opportunity to do what most only dream of—to teach for a year in the same classroom with one's most valued mentor. You will enjoy in this book many of the same economic principles he taught then, but you will also sense in this work his infectious enthusiasm and the seductively entertaining teaching style and language I witnessed daily in 2007, and almost three decades before as a student in his class.

Uwe agreed to be my co-professor for two health policy courses. His favorite afternoon seminar by far was one we facilitated together on the ethics of health policy. I, the former heart transplant surgeon, began by introducing the ethical underpinnings of deciding on the day of a transplant which waiting heart recipient patient (who would die within weeks without the surgery) would receive the extremely scarce resource of a donor heart (others would die waiting). Uwe masterfully weaved the parallel macro ethical policy construct of the allocation of limited health resources within a rich country, especially as it impacts the most vulnerable of our society. Distributive ethics—it was the topic with which he began every lesson. And it's the recurrent underlying theme of this book.

Uwe throughout the book reminds us that economics leads us to better understanding, but that wise policymaking should always begin with a forthright and disciplined discussion of ethical underpinnings. He fundamentally believed that in health policy an ethical vision is inherently "baked into health reform proposals." So when we talk health policy, we should not camouflage the critical ethical discussion, but address it right up front.

Uwe describes this work as a primer for readers, national and international alike. It is much more because it gives us the rich and inspiring insight into the man—a man of smart economics, a teacher who makes the complex simple, the policy influencer who begins every talk asking rhetorical questions about distributive social ethics.

In this book, Uwe does what he does so well—takes us on a delightful journey of understanding basic health policy through the eyes of a practical and realistic economist, seasoned by years of study and writing and lecturing and blogging. Uwe was not one to rest quietly in his ivory tower. He traveled the world sharing his ideas, advising other countries. He was "out there," in the community learning and teaching, even serving on the boards of multiple public health companies.

Uwe was a listener—he said it made him a better teacher. Yes, most saw him charismatically and humbly and self-deprecatingly giving a lecture making the complex simple and clear, just as the reader will experience in this book. But I appreciated equally Uwe the gentle and focused listener, always asking questions and probing respectfully. I see him now, tall and slender, with his wavy thick white hair and sparkling eyes that crinkled with his quick smile, patiently listening for hours to the young college student with a harebrained idea late at night, to the DNA scientist on a lakeside in the woods, and to country music artist Zac Brown explaining how he composes his latest song.

In the book, Uwe skillfully walks the reader through most all the current topics that will continue to surface in health policy debates—both around the kitchen table and in the halls of Congress. For example, on today's interest in price transparency—clearly fundamental to consumers and patients making smart choices in the future—he carefully presents both sides of the health reform argument, calling for more accurate price transparency on the one hand, but on the other arguing against high deductibles as a way to encourage more cost-conscious decision making. ("This is a favorite theory among health economists, and certain politicians they inspire, although it is faith-based, resting on data-free analysis.") This push-pull of economic theory and social health care policy is felt throughout the book. He sums it all up in typical memorable fashion when he describes the limitations of the patient as a health consumer: "In effect, they enter that market like blindfolded shoppers pushed into a department store to shop around smartly for whatever item they might want or, in the case of heath care, need."

Uwe loved America. He always said it was because of his experiences as a kid in Germany and his respect for the American soldiers who were so kind to him. But of course it was much deeper than that. It, he told me, was the opportunity this nation gave him to grow and teach. And we all enjoyed the target of much of his wry humor—those poor souls who so naively take for granted what this nation has to offer.

But throughout his life you could sense his dismay, and he comes back to it again and again throughout this work. How could a nation so wonderful and so powerful and so full of resources not have consensus, or at least a majority view, as to a more rational social compact for those less fortunate? In our many speeches together, I would watch many in the audience squirm a bit when he asked his rhetorical question about our values as a people: "To what extent should the better-off members of society be made to be their poorer and sick brothers' and sisters' keepers in health care?"

Whether everyone in the audience agreed with him or not, people of all stripes would leave much wiser and a lot more inspired to at least consider the impact of health care policy on those most vulnerable.

Uwe was proudly bipartisan. He took what he considered the best from both parties and argued from the economic fundamentals for both, but always dressing them heavily with reality and experience—and with humor just to remind us that no one can be right all the time.

Was Uwe conservative or liberal, a Republican or a Democrat? I could never figure it out. For a while after I left the Senate, people would have us speak at conventions as a contrast, me (the former Republican Majority Leader) representing the "right" and Uwe (the German Canadian Ivy League professor) representing the "left." That didn't last long. Halfway through the debate, he would be out-arguing me from the right with market-based principles and choice, leaving me holding the center-left position demanding universal access—just the opposite of where we started the debate!

In this book, Uwe seemingly leans toward being more critical of the Republican policy approaches of 2017. In a more complete compilation of his speeches and blogs, you would find as much critical of the left as of the right. What you will find common to both sets of policy arguments is his underlying deepseated concern for those with fewer resources, coupled with the economic principles driving behavior and choice.

Uwe, though always careful never to overgeneralize politics or pigeonhole politicians, offers a useful construct when thinking about the philosophies and positions of the two political parties. He says that the proposals of Democrats for the most part are most consistent with the values of health care as a "social good," and those of Republicans are most consistent with health care treated as a private consumption good subjected to pricing and ability to pay.

No mention of Uwe can go without a mention of Tsung-Mei Cheng, the wife he adored. And if you are one of the tens of thousands of people who heard his public lectures over the years, you likely know her as well because almost without exception he took a minute or five or ten of every talk to share something about the love of his life and the enabling and sustaining impact, both personal and professional, she had on his life and values. They were truly one.

And although this book is not about the clinical side of health delivery, I feel obliged to share, as Uwe would in conversation so often, how much he championed the on-the-ground health worker—the community worker, the nurse, the medical student, the doctor. He felt that our fragmented, chaotic financial delivery system entrapped them in a way that unfairly restricted their ability to serve.

Uwe would close each talk with self-deprecating humor. Such humor surfaces throughout the book. It's as if he is saying, "Learn all you can, grasp the economic fundamentals, factor in your own views on ethical construct—but then just step back and decide for yourself what is the right thing to do." By the way, as he says with a smile to keep it all in perspective, economics as a profession is an "academic discipline that is as much ideology practiced in the guise of science as it is actual science."

My last review of this manuscript with Uwe was in the redwood forests that he loved so much north of San Francisco. He shared it with our campmates around a blazing campfire, probing for their critiques and suggestions. His audience was broad and from all walks of life—as Uwe always liked it—writers, executives, engineers, musicians, artists, entrepreneurs, and retirees. The sparring, the self-deprecating humor, the deep respect for economic principles, the wry smile, the quizzical look, the laughter—he captures the moment and educates so seamlessly.

Would I have become a doctor without early exposure to Uwe? Certainly. Would I have become a senator? Probably. But would I have so strongly considered caring for the underserved as I did in my clinical years, or dedicated much of my political influence in Washington to the writing and passage of PEPFAR, the public health legislation led by President George W. Bush, that has contributed to saving over twenty million lives of those with HIV, mostly from the poorest nations in the world? Of course, there is no real answer, but in my gut I feel I would have approached my vocations with less compassion for my fellow man were it not for Uwe.

What I can say for certain is that Uwe's unwavering central organizing philosophy—which I heard first almost five decades ago as his student, taught by his side ten years ago, and have shared with my own colleagues in health policy over the years—has been foundational to my clinical career as a physician, my political and policy years, and, for the past decade, building health care organizations: "Should the child of a poor American family have the same chance of avoiding preventable illness or of being cured from a given illness as does the child of a rich American family?"

Uwe Reinhardt . . . the master teacher.

PROLOGUE

More and more Americans today are finding that health care has become increasingly expensive and, for many, unaffordable. Compared to national health systems in the rest of the developed world, American health care and the American health system are exceedingly complex and almost beyond human comprehension. As America faces such a crossroads where we must decide how we should proceed with our health care and health reform going forward, the need to understand both is great, especially now.

Unfortunately, we are too shy in this country to debate forthrightly the ethical precepts we would like to see imposed on our health care system. It can fairly be said that this shyness is particularly evident on the right of the ideological spectrum—among Americans who would prefer to see health care rationed at least to some extent by price and ability to pay, that is, by income class.

To illustrate, after a reading of H.R. 1628, the American Health Care Act (AHCA) of 2017, the leading health care reform proposal in the first half of 2017 intended to repeal and replace the Affordable Care Act (popularly known as Obamacare) and passed by the U.S. House of Representatives, can anyone doubt that Speaker of the House Paul Ryan (R-WI), chief architect of the act, favored the rationing of health care (beyond a bare-bones level) by income class? How else can one interpret the estimated impact of the bill on American families?

Yet can we imagine Speaker Ryan ever stating his revealed preference in this regard openly on a Sunday morning talk show or on the campaign trail? It seems entirely fair, however, to hold him to the famous dictum of President Nixon's attorney general, John Mitchell: "Watch what we do, not what we say."[1]

My personal experience is that merely bringing up the topic of distributive social ethics for health care can easily raise the ire of an audience, because it is viewed as "too personal," "too political," and "too divisive." So instead, we prefer to discuss health reform mainly in technical terms—usually economic ones—and let social ethics fall where they may.

To illustrate this point I cite an article[2] I published in the *Journal of the American Medical Association* (JAMA) in 1997, after the spectacular failure of the Clinton Health Reform Plan. The article was entitled "Wanted: A Clearly Articulated Social Ethic for American Health Care." In its opening paragraph, I raised the following simple question:

> As a matter of national policy, and to the extent that a nation's health system can make it possible, should the child of a poor American family have the same chance of avoiding preventable illness or of being cured from a given illness as does the child of a rich American family?

University of Chicago Distinguished Law Professor Richard Epstein used a solidly Libertarian theory of justice to answer my question with a clear no. So charmed was I by this forthright response that I arranged a debate with him before some 500 University of Chicago students and faculty, followed by a cordial lunch from which we departed as friends who respectfully agreed to disagree with each other.

Remarkably, but not surprisingly, all five physicians who wrote letters to JAMA on my article failed to answer my simple question. Instead, they furiously went ad hominem, writing me off as a "socialist propagandist"—merely for raising a question that every thoughtful person should be able to answer.

In May 2017, late-night host and comedian Jimmy Kimmel, who answered my question in the affirmative in his emotional plea[3] for universal health care after his son was born with a congenital heart defect, was told by a conservative columnist, "Shut up, Jimmy Kimmel, you elitist creep."[4] It was par for the course.

This taboo on explicitly raising questions on social ethics in health care is of the same kindred spirit that now drives so many college students to stifle debates on topics that make them feel uncomfortable. It is nothing new in American culture. None other than Alexis de Tocqueville remarked on this cultural trait in chapter 15 of his book *Democracy in America* (1835), where he delivered himself of the following passage:

> I know of no country in which there is so little independence
> of mind and freedom of discussion as in America.

Tocqueville noted that anyone going beyond the barriers of political correctness established by the "tyranny of the majority" would not face jail or death by auto-da-fé. The First Amendment of the U.S. Constitution protects us from that fate. However, persons stepping outside those barriers, writes Tocqueville, will find themselves ostracized socially, politically, and economically. We see it on our campuses today. We see it almost daily as individuals lose their jobs over just one slip of the tongue judged politically incorrect. We also see it in our ever so polite "national conversations" on health reform, which judiciously overlook the elephant in the room and write off with unflattering labels those who do want to talk about that elephant.

Not surprisingly, our national health policy is a bundle of confusion and contradictions.

We tacitly expect our doctors, nurses, and other providers of health care to conduct their clinical practices in strictly *egalitarian* terms, that is, to treat health care as purely a *social good*. Imagine the outcry in the media, and especially in hyperventilating hearings in Congress or state legislatures, if a hospital had one lavishly furnished wing for privately insured patients and another bare-bones wing for patients covered by Medicaid or the uninsured.[5]

In late 2016, the CEO of the Mayo Clinic mentioned in a speech to employees[6] that henceforth the Mayo Clinic would give privately insured patients priority over Medicaid patients. It took but a few days of outrage in the media and among government officials[7] to force him to backpedal.[8] His remark was a rational response to an economic signal flashed to him by state legislators who set fees for Medicaid far below those for commercial health insurance. Alas, it was not politically correct.

Yet, while we hold doctors, hospitals, and other providers of health care to strictly *egalitarian* standards, we routinely signal through our payment systems that, in our eyes, the value of the professional work of doctors, and of hospital staffs varies by the socioeconomic status of the patient. New Jersey, for example, pays a pediatrician only about a third as much for a poor child on Medicaid as he or she is paid for a commercially insured child. New Jersey legislators literally signal to pediatricians that their professional work is worth three times as much or more when applied to a commercially insured child than it is when applied to a poor child covered by Medicaid. In this respect, New Jersey legislators (and those of other states) adhere to the Code of Hammurabi[9] (1754 BC), which included a schedule of physician fees (codes 215 to 223) that increased with the socioeconomic status of the patient (slave, freedman, and nobleman).[10]

And so, permanently reluctant ever to debate openly the distributive social ethic that should guide our health system, with many Americans thoroughly confused on the issue, we shall muddle through health reform, as we always have in the past, and as we always shall for decades to come. Our doctors, nurses, and research scientists will work hard to bring about many wondrous cures on the *clinical facet* of our health system, while the *financial facet* will forever remain a fount of rancor, confusion, litigation, and political posturing.

It must be disillusioning for our clinical health workers to be embedded in such a system.

This book is a primer for readers who are interested in our confusing debate on health reform and our health system in general. The book seeks to shed light on important and often bizarre and curious facts and realities about the many facets of our mysterious and expensive health care system. For international readers, I hope the book will offer takeaway lessons from the American experience, especially with regard to what *not* to do in the health care and health reform in their respective countries.

Finally, a note on a few of the terms mentioned above, dealing with the areas of health care we will be looking at in the book. The term "health system" includes three distinct facets, to wit:

1. the *clinical facet* of actual health care production and delivery;
2. the *economic facet* by which health care is financed; and
3. the *regulatory facet*, which provides the administrative structure of the health system.

Were the book focused on the clinical facet of our health system, its tone would be more upbeat and optimistic on the future. The clinical facet of our health system is highly innovative, promising many future clinical breakthroughs and improvements in the safety and quality of care. In its clinical facet, the U.S. health system, although not perfect, probably is unrivaled in the world. Some clinical experts, however, have argued that even on this facet "there is broad consensus that the quality of care that is delivered in the United States is uneven and too often inadequate.[11]

Many of the provisions of the Affordable Care Act of 2010 (Obamacare) did seek to enhance the quality and efficiency of the clinical facet of our health system. The health reforms discussed more recently in 2017, however, focused mainly on the regulatory and financial facets of the system. Therefore, so will this book. Unfortunately, here the tone of the discussion will be somber and critical. The manner in which we finance health care in this country, in particular, is bewildering and inefficient. Elsewhere I have described it as one of chaos behind a veil of secrecy.[12] Indeed, at international conferences on health policy, the U.S. system of financing health care is routinely viewed as the bogeyman of health policy—as an example of how *not* to structure a nation's health system.

I have documented many of the statements in the book with links to supporting research or news reports. The links are in the Notes section of the book. I have also provided many graphs, figures, and charts to give readers an opportunity to take a visual stroll through America's health care wonderland. As the old adage goes, a picture is worth a thousand words.

Uwe E. Reinhardt
Princeton, New Jersey

PRICED

OUT

Introduction

Even twenty years ago, it should have been clear that the collision of two powerful, long-term trends in our economy would eventually drive the debate on U.S. health policy to the impasse it reached in 2017. Indeed, some of us had predicted it years ago. (See, for example, "Is There Hope for the Uninsured?," *Health Affairs* [2003].[1])

The debate is conducted in the jargon of *economics* and *constitutional federal-state relations*. But it is not really about economics and the Constitution at all. Instead, at the heart of the debate is a long-simmering argument over the following question on distributive *social ethics*:

> ***To what extent should the better-off members of society be made to be their poorer and sick brothers' and sisters' keepers in health care?***

The two ominous long-term trends on which I based my dire prognosis on the uninsured are the following:

1. the rapid secular growth in the cost of American health care, in the face of
2. the growing inequality[2] in the distribution of income and wealth in this country.

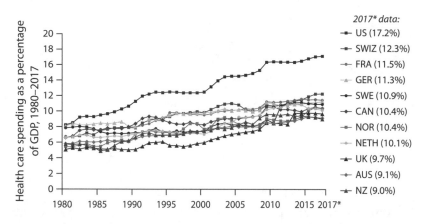

Figure I.1 Health Care Spending as a Percentage of GDP, 1980–2017 (Adjusted for Differences in Cost of Living). Current expenditures on health per capita, adjusted for current US$ purchasing power parities (PPPs). Based on System of Health Accounts methodology, with some differences between country methodologies (data for Australia uses narrower definition for long-term care spending than other countries). *2017 data are provisional or estimated.

Source: Roosa Tikkanen, *Multinational Comparisons of Health Systems Data, 2018* (Commonwealth Fund, Dec. 2018), https://www.commonwealthfund.org/publications /publication/2018/dec/multinational-comparisons-health-systems-data-2018.

Figures I.1 and I.2 give a sense of these two trends.

Over time, these two trends have combined to price a growing number of American families out of the high-quality or at least luxurious American health care that families in the higher strata of the nation's income distribution would like to have for themselves. We have now reached a pass where bestowing on a low-income American even standard medical procedures, such as a coronary bypass or a hip replacement, is the financial equivalent of bestowing on a poor patient a fully loaded Mercedes-Benz.

The American people's legendary apathy on such matters (see, for example, Uwe Reinhardt, "Taking Our Gaze away from Bread and Circus Games" [1995])[3] has facilitated the unabated growth of these trends over time.[4] The people's leaders, from

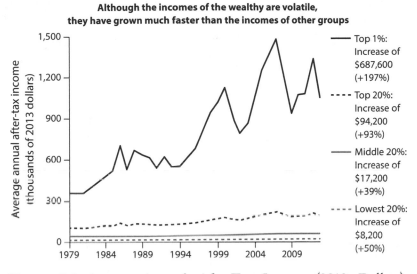

Figure I.2 Average Annual After-Tax Income (2013 Dollars). Increase calculated for 1980–2013.
Source: Congressional Budget Office, *The Distribution of Household Income and Federal Taxes, 2013*, June 2016. Compiled by Peter G. Peterson Foundation, 2016. Reprinted with permission from PGPF.

every incumbent president down,[5] simply told voters that we had the best macro economy in the world, and also the best health system in the world, bar none, and that was good enough for the general populace.

In the early postwar period and through the 1990s, the dream among health policy analysts and the policy makers they advised had been to construct for America a roughly egalitarian, universal health insurance and health care system.

That dream appears to be dead. We will examine the symptoms of its demise throughout the book. Just one example is the ceaseless talk about the economic "sustainability" of Medicare and Medicaid. That argument reflects efforts by some members of Congress and their advisers to construct for the United States an *officially* sanctioned, multi-tier health system in which the quality of health insurance and of the health care experience of low-income and lower-middle-class Americans does not have to match the health care experience of families in the upper strata of the nation's income distribution. In effect, they seek a system in which health care is rationed by income class.

The argument that U.S. spending on Medicare for the elderly and Medicaid for the poor and disabled is not "affordable" or "economically sustainable" seems to have wide currency in the arena of public opinion; but it is a highly dubious argument that calls for quick comment.

Medicare

One should always challenge anyone who declares that a trend—any trend—is "unsustainable" or "not affordable" to explain exactly what he or she means by these words. Usually the response will be vague or plainly *political*, that is, not about economics at all.

To illustrate, figure 1-8 in a 2016 report[6] by the prestigious Medicare Payment Advisory Commission (Medpac) shows that in some years Medicare spending rose faster than private health insurance spending, while in other years it was the other way around. These growth rates are reproduced in figure I.3.

If Medicare spending is not sustainable, is health spending sustainable under private health insurance, whose growth in per capita health spending in many years has exceeded the growth in Medicare spending per beneficiary?

The latest estimates by the Trustees of the Medicare program[7] indicate that Medicare currently accounts for 3.6 percent of gross domestic product (GDP) and will claim 6 percent of GDP by 2050. For 2016, that comes to a claim of 2016 per capita GDP of $2,088, leaving a non-Medicare GDP per capita of about $56,000.

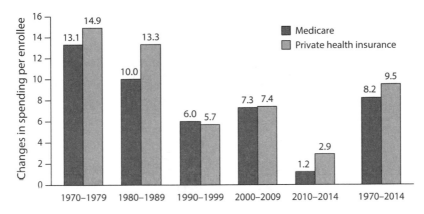

Figure I.3 Changes in Spending per Enrollee, Medicare and Private Health Insurance.
Source: Medicare Payment Advisory Commission (Medpac) Data Book "Health Care Spending and the Medicare Program," June 2016, Figure 1-8.

According to the Congressional Budget Office (CBO), real GDP is expected to grow by only 1.9 percent per year for the foreseeable future (although that number may be higher if promises made by the Trump administration come true). If we subtract from the growth of real GDP the currently projected population growth of about 0.9 percent per year, we conclude that the CBO projects real GDP per capita to grow by about 1 percent. At an annual compound growth rate of 1 percent, real GDP (in 2017 prices) will be $80,544 in 2050. After a claim of 6 percent, or $4,833, for Medicare, that leaves the contemporaries living in 2050 with $75,700 of non Medicare GDP per capita. Thus, in 2050 the contemporaries living then will have 35 percent more real *non-Medicare GDP* per capita than we have today.[8] Figure I.4 illustrates these numbers.

So, if we could afford to take care of our elderly in 2016 with a real GDP per capita of only $58,000, why cannot the contemporaries living in 2050 take care of their elderly with a real GDP per capita of $80,500? Put another way, what do pundits and

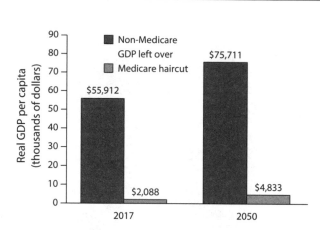

Figure I.4 Real GDP Per Capita after Medicare Haircut, 2017 and 2050. *Source:* Congressional Budget Office, 2017.

politicians who proclaim that Medicare is "unsustainable" mean by that term?

Medicaid

Total Medicaid spending is determined by the number of Americans who are eligible for Medicaid coverage and the amount of spending *per Medicaid enrollee.*

The growth in Medicaid enrollment is driven primarily by the growing income inequality in this country, which tends to increase the number of low-income Americans and with it enrollment in Medicaid, especially during recessions. Indeed, there is now a debate about how long this growing income inequality is politically sustainable, not only in the United States but also in other modern democracies.[9]

The *level* of Medicaid spending *per enrollee* is determined in part (1) by the high cost of U.S. health care in general[10] and (2) by the fact that the Medicaid population tends to be sicker and is more disabled than is the low-income, privately insured population. After a careful review of the literature on Medicaid spending, the Kaiser Family Foundation[11] concluded:

> Spending *per enrollee* is lower for Medicaid compared to private insurance after controlling for differences in socio-demographic and health characteristics between the two groups. Given the significant health and disability differences between Medicaid enrollees and those who are privately insured, the most rigorous research examining differences in *per-enrollee* spending has focused primarily on regression-adjusted comparisons that control for these underlying differences in the need for health care. (Italics added.)

There are no proposals to impose *global* budgets on per capita U.S. health spending in general. In the Congressional Republican reform proposals of 2017, on the other hand, spending on the poor and disabled in Medicaid is to be constrained by converting the current federal assistance to Medicaid, Federal Medical Assistance Percentages (FMAP),[12] into a block grant or per capita cap arrangement whose future growth is to be constrained to the growth merely of the urban Consumer Price Index. That index, however, has always risen more slowly over time than overall per capita health spending in the United States, as figure I.5 shows.

An argument often made by the proponents of constraining Medicaid spending in this way is that actually we are not talking about real cuts, but merely cuts from some imaginary projected future spending path. First, the argument goes, the data are already adjusted for future growth in Medicaid enrollment, because future Medicaid spending is anchored in a block grant. Second, the argument continues, general price inflation (as measured

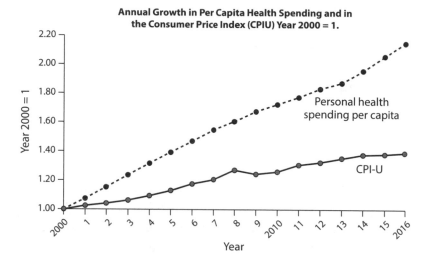

Figure I.5 Annual Growth in Per Capita Health Spending and in the Consumer Price Index (CPIU) Year 2000 = 1.
Sources: For health spending, Department of Human Services (DHHS), Centers for Medicare and Medicaid Services (CMS), "National Health Expenditure Accounts," available at https://www.cms.gov/research-statistics-data-and-systems/statistics-trends-and -reports/nationalhealthexpenddata/nationalhealthaccountshistorical.html. For the infla- tion rate, Inflation Data.com, Tim McMahon, "Historical Consumer Price Index (CPI-U)," October 13, 2017. https://inflationdata.com/Inflation/Consumer_Price_Index/Historical CPI.aspx?reloaded=true. Last viewed October 20, 2017.

by the CPI-U) always does rise, and therefore so will future Medicaid spending per capita. In a nutshell, the argument con- cludes, there will be no future *cuts* to the Medicaid program.

An interesting experiment here would be to see how members of Congress themselves would react if the tough constraints proposed for future per capita Medicaid spending were to be applied also to the public subsidies the federal government routinely grants health insurance for members of Congress and their staff.

Because even after a lively debate on the matter, we will never be able to reach a political consensus on the fundamental question raised above—to what extent we should become our poorer brothers' and sisters' keepers when they fall ill. All that is left for health policy makers is the construction of an administratively more stable multi-tier health care system that facilitates rationing by income class. Chapters 9 and 10 of this book, which examines the various health reform plans debated during the summer of 2017, shed further light on this issue.

That is the long and short of it.

In the rest of the book, I begin with an overview of U.S. health spending and the factors that drive our high health spending. I argue that these spending trends already are pricing more and more American families in the lower part of the nation's income distribution out of health insurance and health care as families in the upper half of the distribution know it. I then focus on a number of bizarre quirks in our health system that are unique to the United States, explain who actually pays for health care in the United States, and explore the question whether from an international perspective Americans get adequate value for their high health spending.

Part II of the book is devoted to the ethical questions that the current situation in the United States raises for health policy makers. I explain the different distributive ethics different nations impose on their health care systems and how the United States is different from the majority of the rich nations in Europe and Asia in that it has never been able to reach a politically dominant consensus on a distributive ethic for American health care. This is followed by an explanation, from an ethical perspective, of the mechanics of commercial health insurance, which accounts for over a third of the total health spending in the United States. I then turn to focus on health reforms and the ethical precepts that underlay the reforms in recent years. The book ends with a brief novel proposal of my own for the next health reform in the United States.

I
∎

A Visual Stroll through America's Health Care Wonderland

1

■

U.S. Health Spending and
What Drives It

Many Americans, perhaps most, believe that ours is the best health system in the world, bar none. That belief may rest on the fact that we spend more on health care than does any other developed nation in the Organisation for Economic Co-operation and Development (OECD).

As a percentage of GDP or per capita income, U.S. health spending is by far the highest in the world, even though the U.S. population is among the youngest among the developed nations. In 2016, total national health spending in the United States amounted to $3.4 trillion, a claim of 18.1 percent of U.S. GDP, which then was $18.5 trillion. That claim is projected to reach 20 percent by 2025. No other nation even comes close to ceding that large a slice of its GDP to its health care sector.

The per capita cost of health care in this country has been rising inexorably over the past half century. How inexorable these cost increases are can be gauged by the ease with which drug companies can raise prices, even on long-established brand name products and generics.

Just how high U.S. health spending is, both in terms of total national health spending and per capita, can be seen from the international comparative data in the charts that follow.

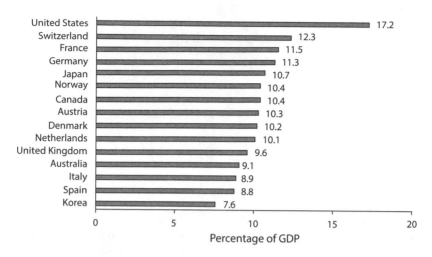

Figure 1.1 Percentage of GDP Claimed by Health Care in Select OECD Countries, 2017.
Source: OECD Data, 2018.

U.S. Health Spending in International Perspective

Figure 1.1 depicts data on total national health spending as a percentage of GDP for 2017 in wealthy countries in the OECD.[1]

The OECD excludes from "health spending" certain items included in the health spending data assembled and published by the Centers for Medicare and Medicaid Services (CMS) of the U.S. Department of Health and Human Services (DHHS). Therefore, the OECD numbers are slightly lower than those published by the CMS, but the relative magnitude of spending among nations is indicative.

U.S. health spending per capita in 2017 amounted to an estimated average of $10,209—about twice as much as is spent per capita in most of the rest of the developed countries. The major exception is GDP-rich Switzerland, whose per capita health

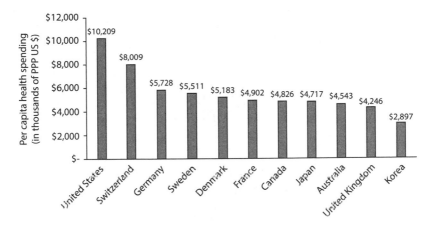

Figure 1.2 Per Capita Health Spending in PPP US $s, Select OECD Countries, 2017.
Source: OECD Data, 2018.

spending is about 78 percent of the U.S. average. Figure 1.2, based on 2017 data reported by the OECD, exhibits these differences in per capita health spending.

What Factors Drive U.S. Health Spending to These High Levels?

It is natural to ask what factors drive the much higher health expenditures in the United States relative to those in other OECD countries. This chapter will focus on the factors that might explain the extraordinarily high level of U.S. health spending. Let us explore the following factors:

A. ability to pay, as measured by real GDP per capita;
B. the demographic structure of the U.S. population;

C. the high prices of U.S. health care; and

D. the huge administrative burden loaded onto medical bills by the extraordinary complexity of our health insurance system.

Ability to Pay as an Explanatory Factor

Our higher GDP per capita means we have a higher ability to pay for goods and services, including health care goods and services, than poorer countries with a lower GDP per capita. Health care goods and services, however, differ from normal goods and services in the economy in one important respect. Economists describe health care as a "superior good." This means that spending on health care tends to rise disproportionately with income. If, for example, in a given year GDP rises by, say, 5 percent, then typically health spending will rise by more than 5 percent, possibly with a lag of a year or two.

If we plot, for a given year, health spending per capita in purchasing power parity U.S. dollars (hereafter PPP US $s) on GDP per capita (ability to pay), also in PPP US $s, we should not be surprised to find a positive bivariate correlation and a so-called income elasticity (percentage change in health spending over percentage change in GDP) in excess of 1.

Figure 1.3 shows that GDP per capita does drive health spending systematically; but that variable alone leaves much unexplained. Even after adjusting the health spending data for GDP per capita (roughly, "ability to pay" for health care), U.S. spending levels are much higher than would be predicted by the trend line. Factors other than GDP per capita must drive U.S. health spending.

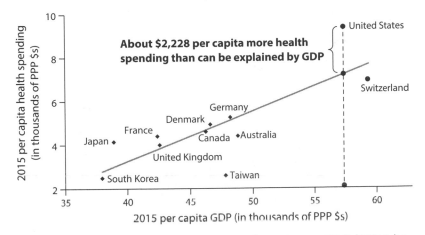

Figure 1.3 Per Capita Health Spending and Per Capita GDP (PPP $s) in Select OECD Countries and Taiwan in 2015.
Source: OECD Health Data, 2016. Data for Taiwan from MOHW, Taiwan, 2016.

Demographic Structure

On average, per capita health spending in any country first falls and then rises with age. It is so in any country, although the spending curve plotted on age varies a bit among countries.

Perhaps surprisingly, the age composition of the population is not a significant factor.

For the United States, the age-spending curve as shown in figure 1.4[2] is indicative. Within the cohort of the elderly above age sixty-five, the spending ratio increases further above 5.31 with age, although that is not shown in the figure.

Thus, one's intuition forged by this chart suggests that per capita health spending in countries with older populations is apt to be higher than that in countries with younger populations. Similarly, one would expect that the aging of the population within a country—for example, the retiring of the baby boom generation in the United States—must be a powerful driver of

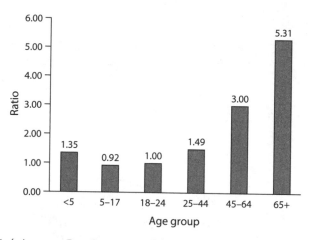

Figure 1.4 Average Per Capita Health Spending in Age Group Relative to Spending by Age Group 18–24 (=1).
Source: http://www.kff.org/report-section/health-care-costs-a-primer-2012-report/.

annual increases in total per capita health spending, averaged over all age groups.

Is that actually so? Perhaps surprisingly, the answer seems to be no, as can be inferred from figure 1.5.

AGING AND HEALTH SPENDING ACROSS COUNTRIES

As figure 1.5 shows, there is a wide variance of spending per capita at any population-age level. The U.S. population is, on average, much younger than the populations of many other countries in the OECD, yet we spend so much more per capita on health care. In fact, although the United States has one of the youngest populations among developed nations, we have the world's highest health spending per capita. Japan, in contrast, has the oldest population but among the lowest health spending levels.

It can be fun to impose a trend line on the data points in figure 1.5. That trend line would have a negative slope, suggesting (spuriously) that the aging of a nation's population lowers its per

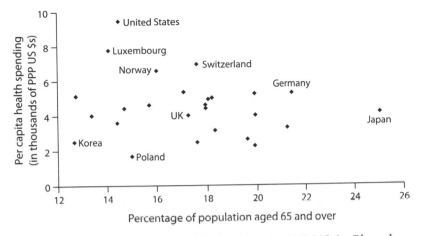

Figure 1.5 2015 Per Capita Health Spending in PPP US $s. Plotted on Percentage of Population Aged 65 and Over.
Source: OECD Data, 2017.

capita health spending. Just two data points would drive that result: the high per capita health spending in the United States, given its relatively young population, and the low health spending per capita in Japan, given its very old population.

Two-dimensional graphs implicitly embody bivariate models with only one explanatory variable and an explained variable. In more elaborate cross-national regression models that control statistically for many other explanatory variables thought to drive health spending, the estimated effect of aging on spending still remains statistically insignificant. It is a curious and counterintuitive fact, but one that should be noted.

AGING AND THE GROWTH OF PER CAPITA HEALTH SPENDING WITHIN COUNTRIES

The aging of the U.S. population often is fingered as a main driver of the annual growth in U.S. health spending. Is that really so?

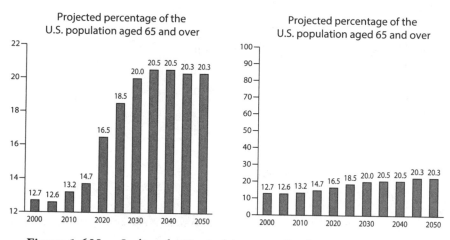

Figure 1.6 How Scaling the Vertical Axes in a Graph Can Easily Trick Its Beholder.
Source: "Does the Aging of the Population Really Drive the Demand For Health Care?," Uwe Reinhardt, *Health Affairs*, 2003, vol. 22, issue 6.

Here the answer is no again, as I have shown in my article "Does the Aging of the Population Really Drive the Demand for Health Care?"[3]

If one assumes (1) that the age-specific, average utilization of health care per capita in dollar terms remains constant at some base-year level (e.g., the year 2000) for the next three or four decades, (2) that the size of the population does not change over that future period, and (3) that the only variable that changes is the age composition of that population, then it will be found that this aging process can explain only about 0.5 percentage points of the usual annual growth of 4 to 6 percentage points in total health spending.

And why is this so? Figure 1.6 can explain it.

In the graph on the left of the chart, the vertical axis goes only from 12 percent to 22 percent. That is the graph commonly presented in connection with the baby boom tsunami. In a graph with the vertical axis running from 0 percent to 100 percent (the

one on the right of the chart), the much-feared baby boom tsunami becomes just a ripple. It shows, as the above-cited paper
does, that the aging of a population is just too small and too grad-
ual a process from year to year to act as a major driver of the
annual growth of U.S. health spending.

Furthermore, we may note in passing that the United States,
along with Canada and Australia, is expected to be forever
younger than the rest of the developed world, including some
Asian countries (e.g., Japan, China, Korea, and Taiwan). For
Americans this should be cheerful news.

The High Price of U.S. Health Care

What, then, does drive the higher U.S. GDP-adjusted health
spending? With the exception of a few high-tech procedures,
Americans actually consume fewer real health care services
(visits with physicians, hospital admissions and hospital days
per admission, medications, and so on) than do Europeans. In
this regard, the reader is referred to a widely quoted paper published in 2003 in the health policy journal *Health Affairs*, entitled "It's the Prices, Stupid: Why the United States Is So
Different from Other Countries."[4] However, earlier publica-
tions made the same point, among them a McKinsey study, to
be discussed further on, and published work by the health
economist Mark Pauly.[5]

For better or for worse—better for the supply side of the health
care sector and worse for consumers—prices for virtually any
health care product or service in the United States tend to be at
least twice as high as those for comparable products or services in
other countries. The International Federation of Health Plans publishes an annual price comparison for standard health care products
and services. That publication is well worth perusing. Figures 1.7
through 1.11 present just some of the data from that comparison.

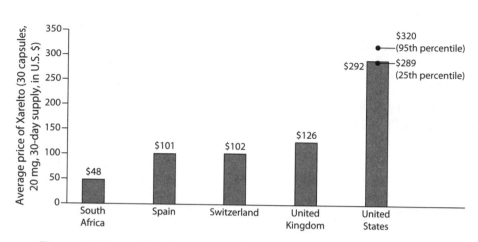

Figure 1.7 Drugs: Xarelto is prescribed to prevent or treat blood clots.
Source: IFHP 2015 Comparative Price Report, published by the International Federation of Health Plans. Reprinted here with permission.

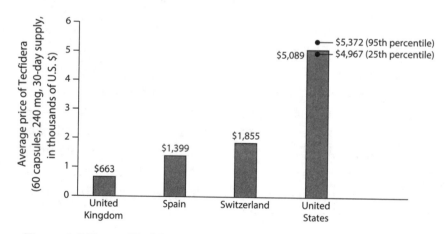

Figure 1.8 Drugs: Tecfidera is prescribed to treat multiple sclerosis.
Source: IFHP 2015 Comparative Price Report, published by the International Federation of Health Plans. Reprinted here with permission.

Prices for health care are instrumental in determining the claim that the health system can stake on GDP. Relative to other countries, prices in the United States make the providers of health care better off and the users of health care worse off. It is

Figure 1.9 Total Hospital and Physician: Appendectomy.
Source: IFHP 2015 Comparative Price Report, published by the International Federation of Health Plans. Reprinted here with permission.

a matter of income distribution on which economists do not have much to say.

The High Administrative Overhead Cost of U.S. Health Care

No other country among the developed economies spends nearly as much on administrative overhead for health care as does the United States, where, before the Affordable Care Act came along, administration absorbed an estimated 25 percent to 30 percent of total health spending. As will be seen further on, the implementation of the Affordable Care Act changed the situation for the better.

Most nations have relatively simple health insurance systems. Usually there is a heavily government-regulated social insurance scheme covering 90 percent to 95 percent of the population, with uniform fee schedules and rules, and a small private insurance market outside the social insurance scheme used by high-income households. The uniformity of fee schedules and rules furnishes

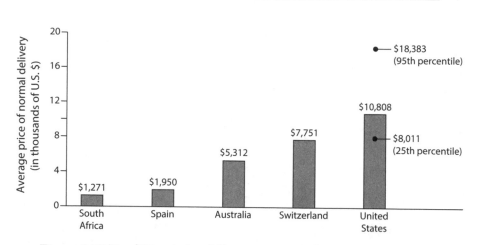

Figure 1.10 Total Hospital and Physician: Normal Delivery.
Source: IFHP 2015 Comparative Price Report, published by the International Federation of Health Plans. Reprinted here with permission.

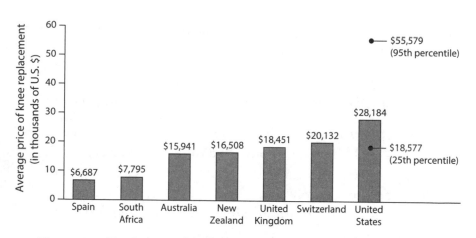

Figure 1.11 Total Hospital and Physician: Knee Replacement.
Source: IFHP 2015 Comparative Price Report, published by the International Federation of Health Plans. Reprinted here with permission.

ideal platforms for the smart application of health information technology (HIT), which can lower administrative costs.

By comparison, the U.S. health insurance system is highly complex, with myriad insurance schemes that vary by the

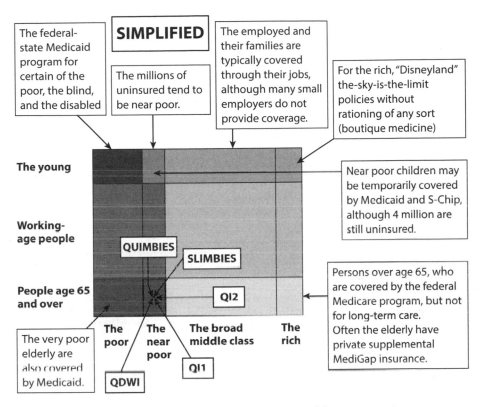

Figure 1.12 Categories of People in the U.S. Health Insurance System

socioeconomic and demographic status of the insured and by employer for families covered by employer-sponsored insurance.

Figure 1.12 conveys the idea. Consider, for example, how many different insurance schemes there are for near-poor elderly Americans.

A health insurance system this complex makes incremental health reform challenging. Changing the rules in one cell of the system can easily have an effect on other cells in the system.

For example, establishing a new public health insurance program for working people whose employers do not offer them

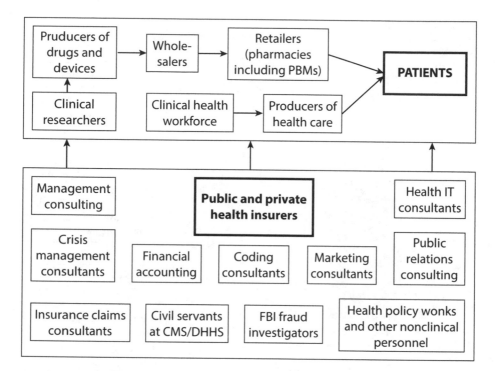

Figure 1.13 The Value Chain in U.S. Health Care, Clinical Enterprise.

health insurance might easily induce employers who now do offer insurance to drop it and load their employees onto the new public program. This phenomenon can significantly raise the budget cost per originally intended object of compassion— sometimes so high that it helps kill the proposed legislation.

If one were to depict a so-called value chain for U.S. health care, it would look something like what is shown in figure 1.13.

The *clinical facet* of the system is shown at the top of the chart. It is supported by a huge armada of nonclinical individuals, shown at the bottom of the chart. Each member of that administrative armada believes itself to be adding "value" to the patient, who must pay for these camp followers' often-handsome

Figure 1.14 The All-American Health Care Team.
Source: Andriy Popov, © 123RF.com.

sustenance. It is not always clear, however, what value patients actually derive from these myriad camp followers.

Figure 1.14 gives a picture of the all-American health care team—more consultants than clinicians.

In an analysis of the growth of the U.S. health workforce over the period 1990–2012, Robert Kocher, MD, of Venrock Capital (formerly of the McKinsey Global Institute, with a detour through the Obama administration) wrote in the *Harvard Business Review*:

> My colleagues and I found that from 1990 to 2012, the number of workers in the U.S. health system grew by nearly 75 percent. Nearly 95 percent of this growth was in non-doctor workers. . . . So, what are all these people doing? Today, for every doctor, only 6 of the 16 non-doctor workers have clinical roles, including registered nurses, allied health professionals, aides, care coordinators, and medical assistants.

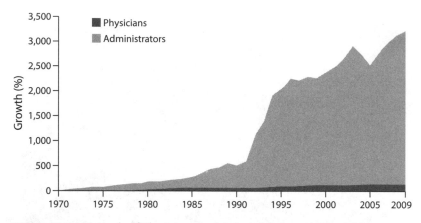

Figure 1.15 Growth of Physicians and Administrators, 1970–2009.
Source: Bureau of Labor Statistics; NCHS; and Himmelstein/Woolhandler analysis of CPS.

Surprisingly, 10 of the 16 non-doctor workers are purely administrative and management staff, receptionists and information clerks, and office clerks. The problem with all of the non-doctor labor is that most of it is not primarily associated with delivering better patient outcomes or lowering costs.[6] (Italics added.)

Figure 1.15 is a famous chart well known to many doctors.

PRIVATE INSURERS

According to a recent publication[7] by America's Health Insurance Plans (AHIP), private health insurers on average take a haircut of about 17.8 percent off the insurance premiums paid by employers or individuals for "operating costs," which means marketing and administration. Another 2.7 percent goes for profits. That haircut was as high as 45 percent pre-Obamacare for smaller insurers selling policies in the (nongroup) market for individually purchased insurance. Under Obamacare the portion of the premium going to marketing, administration, and profits was constrained to 20 percent for small insurers and to 15 percent for large insurers. Under the Senate's 2017 draft bill (The Better Care Reconciliation Act [BCRA]) states would have the freedom to relax these standards.

Some students of administrative costs of Blue Cross Blue Shield plans and other private insurers report that the AHIP number is too high. They currently estimate the range to be between about 9 percent for the Blues and between 10 percent and 11 percent for other private insurers.[8]

PUBLIC INSURANCE PROGRAMS

Government-run health insurance programs do not have marketing costs and profits, and they tend to have low administrative costs as a percentage of their spending for health care. On the other hand, with a never-ending stream of new, arcane regulations that require consultants for interpretation, they impose considerable administrative costs on doctors, hospitals, and other providers of health care.

However, the haircut private and public insurers take off the insurance premium and taxes is only part of the overall administrative overhead of our health system. It probably is not the largest part.

HOSPITALS

Hospitals in other countries may have fewer than half a dozen billing clerks and coding consultants. By contrast, U.S. hospitals require hundreds and thousands of billing clerks. Duke University's health system, for example, with 957 beds, has 1,600 billing clerks.[9]

PHYSICIANS

It is estimated that the typical American physician spends over $80,000 per year interacting with health insurers. That is nearly

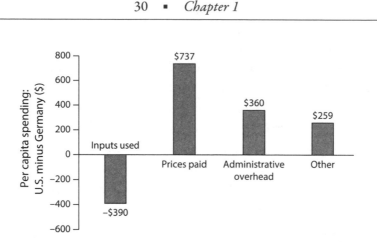

Figure 1.16 Sources of Differences in Health Spending in U.S. Purchasing Power Parity: Per Capita Spending U.S. minus Germany, 1990. Total U.S. $2,439, total Germany $1,373.
Source: http://www.mckinsey.com/industries/healthcare-systems-and-services/our-insights/health-care-productivity.

four times as much as is spent by colleagues in Canada and undoubtedly multiple times what physicians spend in Europe, Taiwan, Japan, and Korea.

In their paper "U.S. Physician Practices versus Canadians: Spending Nearly Four Times as Much Money Interacting with Payers,"[10] the authors write:

> We estimated physician practices in Ontario spent $22,205 per physician per year interacting with Canada's single-payer agency—just 27 percent of the $82,975 per physician per year spent in the United States. US nursing staff, including medical assistants, spent 20.6 hours per physician per week interacting with health plans—nearly ten times that of their Ontario counterparts.

PATIENTS

None of the empirical estimates on administrative expense includes the value of the time American consumers devote to choosing health insurance products or, as patients, to process usually incomprehensible medical bills from the providers of health care or claims from health insurers. Patients who can afford it can hire billing consultants who front for them when querying medical bills.

Elisabeth Rosenthal,[11] formerly of the *New York Times* and now at the Kaiser Family Foundation, describes in her article on medical bills that doctors and hospitals contract with armies of coding specialists to help them code their work in a way that extracts the maximum revenue from the rest of society (private and public insurers as well as patients). For their part, private insurers contract with equally adept coding experts to help them fend off up-coding by providers of care. There is nothing like this unproductive zero-sum game in the rest of the world.

The enormous administrative overhead in U.S. health care had been noted as early as the 1990s by the McKinsey Global Institute. Figure 1.16 is based on a very sophisticated study published by the institute in 1996, based on data for 1990 gathered by the study.

As this chart indicates, in 1990 Americans actually used $390 less in real health services per capita (both priced out at and expressed in U.S. prices) than did Germans.

However, Americans paid $737 more per capita than did Germans in higher prices for identical health care products and services. Furthermore, Americans spent $360 more per capita than did Germans on administrative overhead, and $259 more per capita than did Germans for "other," a category that may have included more administrative expense not specifically identified.

In other words, almost all of the $390 in savings (the McKinsey authors called it higher productivity) squeezed out of American clinicians was absorbed in the United States by added administrative expense. For hardworking American clinicians, this reallocation of the health care dollar must be a source of anger.

All told, Americans in 1990 spent $2,439 per capita on health care—$966 or 65 percent more per capita than did Germans, who spent only $1,473 per capita (both in PPP $s).

Unfortunately, none of the higher U.S. spending represented more consumption of real health services. All of the difference (and more) between American and German health spending represented higher administrative costs, higher prices, and higher spending on "other" non–health care items.

It is anyone's guess what added value American patients and insured consumers derive from the huge overhead they must finance. One can only hope that whatever that added value may be, it covers the enormous cost of that system. Alas, that is open to doubt. To quote Henry Aaron, the distinguished health economist at the Brookings Institution, in a commentary published in the *New England Journal of Medicine*:

> I look at the U.S. health care system and see an administrative monstrosity, a truly bizarre mélange of thousands of payers with payment systems that differ for no socially beneficial reason, as well as staggeringly complex public systems with mind-boggling administered prices and other rules expressing distinctions that can only be regarded as weird.[12]

OUR EXPENSIVE DRUG DISTRIBUTION SYSTEM

Spending on prescription drugs has become the fastest-growing component of total health spending in the United States. This is so because, as was noted earlier, Americans pay much higher prices for a given drug than do citizens of other developed countries. Furthermore, drug manufacturers in recent years have been able to raise prices substantially, even for long-established generic products. It has prompted President Trump to declare that the pharmaceutical industry is "getting away with murder."[13]

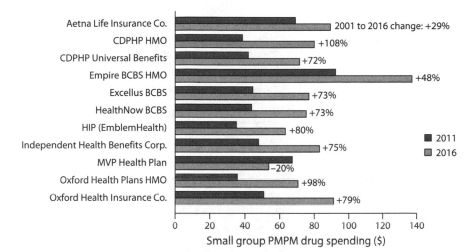

Figure 1.17 Small Group PMPM Drug Spending, 2011 and 2016.
Source: United Hospital Fund analysis of 1) Statement of Revenue and Expenses by Line of Business, New York Supplements to the National Association of Insurance Commissioners Annual Statements, filed with the NYS Department of Financial Services by nine health plans participating in the small group market, for calendar years 2011 and 2016; 2) for Aetna Life Insurance Company, 2016 New York State Supplement, and for 2011, Medical Loss Ratio Reporting Form filed with the U.S. Department of Health and Human Services, small group market; and 3) for HealthNow New York, small group market prescription drug data obtained through personal communication with the insurer. Newell P. and S. R. Hefter. June 2017. Under Pressure: Prescription Drug Spending Trends in New York's Medicaid Program and Small Group Market. New York: United Hospital Fund. https://uhfnyc.org/publications /881226.

Recently the United Hospital Fund of New York undertook a study[14] on spending on prescription drugs per insured member per month registered by a number of health insurance plans in New York State. Figures 1.17 and 1.18 are two graphics presented in the study.

In their defense, drug manufacturers[15] explain that the high cost of prescription drugs is partly the result of an elaborate and expensive drug distribution system. Figures 1.19 and 1.20 are from a paper[16] presented at a seminar sponsored by the Brookings Institution in June 2017.

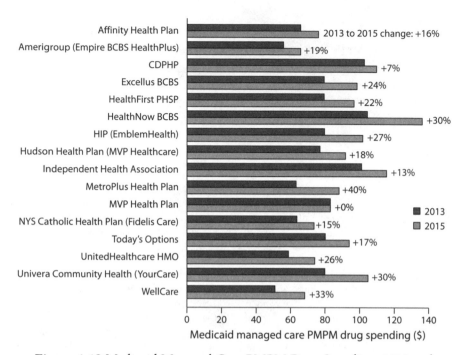

Figure 1.18 Medicaid Managed Care PMPM Drug Spending, 2013 and 2015.

Source: United Hospital Fund analysis of 1) Statement of Revenue and Expenses by Line of Business, New York Supplements to the National Association of Insurance Commissioners Annual Statements, filed with the NYS Department of Financial Services by nine health plans participating in the small group market, for calendar years 2011 and 2016; 2) for Aetna Life Insurance Company, 2016 New York State Supplement, and for 2011, Medical Loss Ratio Reporting Form filed with the U.S. Department of Health and Human Services, small group market; and 3) for HealthNow New York, small group market prescription drug data obtained through personal communication with the insurer. Newell P. and S. R. Hefter. June 2017. Under Pressure: Prescription Drug Spending Trends in New York's Medicaid Program and Small Group Market. New York: United Hospital Fund. https://uhfnyc.org/publications/881226.

Figure 1.19 shows the nature of the drug distribution system, although in real life it is even more complicated than that. For example, some Pharmaceutical Benefit Managers (PBMs) also function as retail pharmacies.

Figure 1.20 shows the authors' estimates of the cut each agent in the value chain from producing prescription drugs to consumer

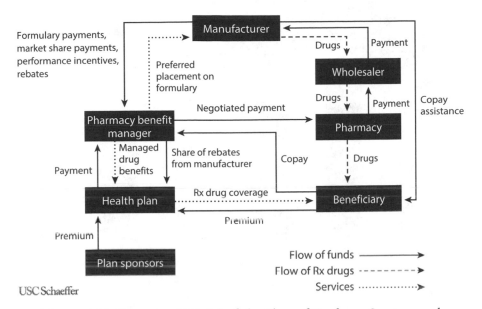

Figure 1.19 Conceptual Model of the Flow of Products, Services, and Funds for Nonspecialty Drugs Covered under Private Insurance and Purchased in a Retail Setting.
Source: Sood N., Shih T., Van Nuys K., and Goldman D. (2017). The Flow of Money through the Pharmaceutical Distribution System. USC Leonard D. Schaeffer Center for Health Policy & Economics White Paper, figure 1.

spending on drugs (out of pocket or as part of a health insurance premium) takes from that money flow. The chart shows that drugs that cost $17 to produce end up costing patients or purchasers of health insurance $100.

Of a total $100 in consumer spending, health insurers pay PBMs $81, keeping $19 for themselves, of which $3 is profit; the rest goes for marketing and administration.

PBMs are supposed to manage prescription drugs for health insurers. That task includes negotiating prices with drug manufacturers and dealing with retail pharmacies and patients. The PBMs pay pharmacies $76, keeping $5, of which $2 is profit. Of the $76 the retail pharmacies receive from the PBMs and co-pays paid by patients, they keep $15, of which $3 is profit. The retail

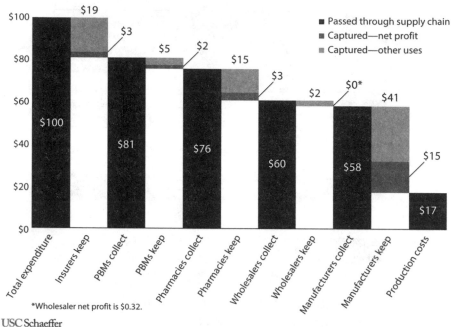

Figure 1.20 Flow of a Hypothetical $100 Expenditure on Prescription Drugs Covered under Private Insurance through the U.S. Retail Distribution System.
Source: Sood N., Shih T., Van Nuys K., and Goldman D. (2017). The Flow of Money through the Pharmaceutical Distribution System. USC Leonard D. Schaeffer Center for Health Policy & Economics White Paper, figure 2.

pharmacies pay pharmaceutical wholesalers roughly $60; they in turn pay manufacturers $58. Manufacturers spend $17 for manufacturing the drugs and $26 for marketing, administration, and research and development (R&D); they keep $15 as profit, a handsome net profit margin of 26 percent. In general, research-based drug manufacturers spend about twice as much on marketing and administration as on R&D.

Total profits alone booked by all of the agents in the value chain collectively amount to $23 of the $100 paid for drugs by consumers.

Although PBMs claim to be able to drive tough bargains with drug manufacturers and retail pharmacies over prescription drug prices, they seem to have only a modest capacity to do so. First, as can be inferred from data published by the International Federation of Health Plans, the prices Americans pay for drugs are the highest in the world. Second, the PBMs seem unable to resist the steep annual price increases for existing drugs that drug companies routinely manage to impose on them, even generic ones. In early June 2017, for example, it was widely reported[17] that Pfizer had raised prices on ninety-one existing drugs by an average of 20 percent since the beginning of 2017. There is a good chance that the PBMs will just accept such increases and pay them.

Insured patients typically are required to pay at the pharmacy coinsurance pegged to the price their PBM has negotiated with retail pharmacies. But the PBMs receive from the drug manufacturers secret rebates that, so claim the PBMs, are mostly passed on to the health insurers with whom they contract, who in turn claim to pass most of the secret rebates on to the employers with whom they contract. Given this secret rebate flow, one wonders what incentives the PBMs actually have to help keep drug prices low for consumers.

Probably nothing so clearly exposes the disregard for efficiency and costs with which Congress sometimes fashions health policy than the distribution of drugs for cancer and rheumatology treatments. These drugs commonly are administered on an ambulatory basis in the medical practices of oncologists and rheumatologists or in outpatient departments of hospitals.

Under the Medicare program, a major payer for these drugs, physicians and hospital outpatient departments are reimbursed by Medicare for the drugs they infuse at the Average Sales Price (ASP) for the drugs reported by the drug industry to Medicare, plus a 6 percent markup over the ASP. With some of these drugs costing more than $100,000 a year, this 6 percent markup clearly provides a strong financial incentive for physicians to favor expensive drugs.

One would hope that in their clinical decisions most physicians would be impervious to this strong financial incentive. It was troubling, however, to behold the vehement opposition[18] on the part of the American medical community, the pharmaceutical industry, and members of Congress who front for the pharmaceutical industry to a proposal by the Innovation Center of the Centers for Medicare and Medicaid (CMS) to experiment with alternative payment approaches.

The idea was to reduce the percentage markup on cancer and rheumatology drugs from 6 percent to 2.5 percent and to increase the flat fee paid physicians and hospital outpatient departments for administering the drugs. That sensible idea had been recommended[19] to CMS by the nonpartisan Medicare Payment Advisory Commission (Medpac).

In the face of this vehement opposition from powerful interest groups and from the members of Congress who carry their water, CMS in late December 2016 simply abandoned the idea of reforming this conflict-ridden drug reimbursement system. On behalf of the interest groups, K Street lobbyists won out over plain common economic sense.

THE ROLE OF CONGRESS IN DRIVING UP ADMINISTRATIVE EXPENSES

I can think of no legislation ever to emerge from Congress that addressed the magnitude of this administrative overhead. It is as if Congress just does not care what health spending by consumers actually buys in America.

On the contrary, every health reform emerging from Congress vastly complicates the system further and brings forth new armadas of nonclinical consultants who make a good living teaching clinicians and hospitals how to cope with the new onslaught of administrative strictures. All of their income becomes the providers' expense and thus ends up in the patient's bill.

A classic illustration of this tendency in Congress is its introduction of so-called Flexible Spending Accounts (FSAs).[20] They allow employed individuals to set aside, at the beginning of the year, out of pretax income, a certain amount of money to cover out-of-pocket spending for health care in the coming year.

As is well known, or should be well known, any expenditure that comes out of pretax income or, which is equivalent, is deductible from taxable income, is just another tax-financed subsidy in disguise.[21] In this case, the larger the employee's income and thus marginal tax rate, the larger that public subsidy.

Tax-preferred Health Savings Accounts (HSAs) are now all the rage. They, too, provide tax-financed public subsidies[22] that favor mainly high-income households. Individuals can deposit money in these savings accounts, out of pretax income, to help defray out-of-pocket spending for health care.[23] HSAs differ from FSAs in that unspent balances in one year carry over to the next year, while unspent balances in FSAs are lost to the employee and revert to the employer.[24]

Aside from being regressive, however, FSAs and HSAs have another dubious claim. These accounts have given rise to yet another profit-seeking new industry[25] of nonclinical "health workers" who feed themselves at the health care trough, which patients must fill with their insurance premiums or out-of-pocket payments. Someone must hold the funds in the HSAs and make sure that the owners of FSAs and HSAs do not charge to these accounts frivolous items not allowed under the legislation authorizing them. This new industry serves those functions.

Presumably, this new industry produces value for taxpayers who use these accounts to shift their tax burden onto the shoulders of other taxpayers, who are the losers from the policy. The industry's revenues are part of GDP, as if it actually produced value for society as a whole. What that value would be, however, is not clear to this economist.

Nevertheless, Congress loves these nonproductive redistributions of tax burden among taxpayers. Tax preferences—properly called "tax expenditures"[26] by economists—are the vehicles for these dubious favors. It is easy to see why Congress loves tax preferences. As *New York Times* op-ed columnist David Brooks has put it in one of his columns:[27]

> David Bradford, a Princeton economist, has the best illustration of how the system [of tax preferences] works. Suppose the Pentagon wanted to buy a new fighter plane. But instead of writing a $10 billion check to the manufacturer, the government just issued a $10 billion "weapons supply tax credit." The plane would still get made. The company would get its money through the tax credit. And politicians would get to brag that they had cut taxes and reduced the size of government!

So it goes. With tax deductibility of expenditures or other forms of tax preference, Congress can provide favorite constituents tax-financed subsidies that do not formally show up as government spending but can even be deceptively styled as tax reductions. Only economists and politicians appear to understand this dubious game.

2

■

Pricing Americans Out
of Health Care

The Milliman Medical Index

How affordable is U.S. health care? The high cost of health care in the United States threatens inexorably to price kindness out of the souls of an otherwise kind people.

To see why millions of Americans are increasingly priced out of health care as we know it, we can confront the so-called Milliman Medical Index (see figure 2.1), which shows data on the distribution of income and wealth in the United States.

The Milliman Medical Index is tracked by the well-known actuarial firm Milliman, which draws on a database of several million insured American families. The index shows *total spending* for health care for a typical American family of four (with ages under sixty-five) covered by employment-based preferred provider organization (PPO) health insurance. "Total spending" in the index is defined as the sum of

a. the employer's contribution to the family's insurance coverage, plus
b. the employee's contribution to the premium for that coverage, plus
c. the family's out-of-pocket spending.

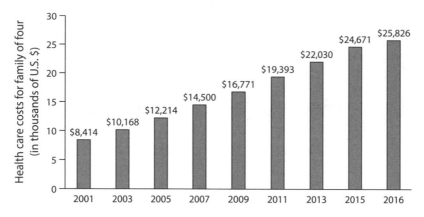

Figure 2.1 Milliman Medical Index of Health Care Cost for Family of Four Covered by Employment-Based PPO, 2016.
Source: http://us.milliman.com/mmi/.

PPO health insurance contracts sponsored by employers are widely regarded as the benchmark for good health insurance in the United States. They are thought to provide the kind of coverage that, ideally, every American should have. Most Americans debating health policy or designing health reform legislation have this form of coverage.

The virtue of the Milliman Index is that it includes *out-of-pocket spending* by families. The current debate on health reform typically focuses only on whether *insurance premiums* rise or fall, as if that were the proper metric for judging the affordability of health care. It is not. Total spending matters.

Figure 2.1 shows the time path of this index from 2001, when it stood at $8,414, to 2016, when it had reached $25,826. For 2017 the index rose again, to $26,944, an increase of $1,118. That number may seem extraordinary, but less so when one recalls that per capita health spending in the United States stood at $10,209 in 2017.

The level of these numbers and their growth over time are remarkable. They suggest that, so far, the private health insurance

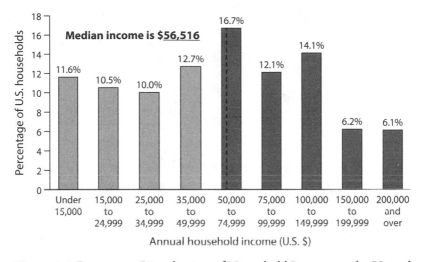

Figure 2.2 Percentage Distribution of Household Income in the United States in 2015.
Source: Data from Statista, 2015.

sector has not been able to control the growth of health spending any better than has the public sector. For both sectors, health care spending has risen apace, although a bit more slowly in the past decade than before.

The Distribution of Income and Wealth in the United States

Now contrast the Milliman Medical Index with the distribution of household income and wealth in the United States, shown in figures 2.2 and 2.3. As figure 2.2 shows, in 2015 the distribution of annual money income[1] of U.S. households had a median of $56,516. Half of U.S. households had a lower income than that. Almost a third had an income of $35,000 or less.

For a U.S. family of four covered by an employment-based PPO contract, about half of the median income of $56,000 would be claimed by health care alone if that family had to cover the annual health spending of $27,000 (2017) out of its own household budget. That median income would not even be

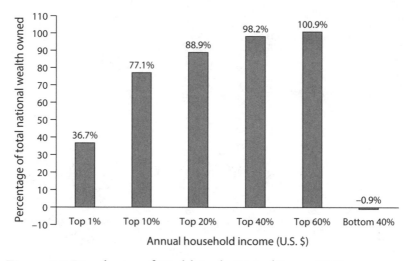

Figure 2.3 Distribution of Wealth in the United States, 2013.
Source: Edward N. Wolff, www.nber.org/papers/w20733.pdf.

enough to cover the annual cost of, say, a new cancer drug or other new biological drugs.

The Stark Choices Confronting U.S. Health Policy Makers

The high and growing cost of U.S. health care, combined with the inequality in the distribution of income and wealth among American families, confronts U.S. health policy makers with the following stark choices:

1. If it is desired that *all* Americans have access to roughly the same kind of health care on terms they can afford with their own, often small household budgets, then purchasing power for health care must be transferred somehow from households in the upper strata of the income distribution to families in the lower strata. There are several mechanisms by which this transfer of money could be achieved.

2. However, if those transfers are politically impossible, then access to health care and its quality must be rationed somehow by income class. This would result in a multitiered health system, with a medical Disneyland for the well-to-do (now called "boutique medicine"[2]) at the top, a bare-bones system for the poor at the bottom, and different tiers in between, depending on patients' ability to pay. For the most part, lower-income American families would be priced out of health care as families in the upper half of the income distribution know it and prefer it.

3. A third alternative would be to copy the approaches used in other countries to control the level and growth of the cost of health care, which would include more uniformity in fee schedules and outright price regulation.

If health policy makers opted for the first choice, they could use several vehicles for transferring money from high- to low-income households, to wit:

1. Explicit taxes and transfers through public budgets.

2. *Community-rated* health insurance premiums that are the same for healthy and sick individuals in large risk pools, thus forcing younger and healthier individuals to subsidize through their premiums the health care of older and sicker individuals.

3. *Price discrimination,* whereby prices for some patients are set high to help finance deep price discounts extended to poor patients or outright charity care.

In the United States we have used all three transfer mechanisms in the past.

The first transfer mechanism—explicit taxes and transfers—is used for Medicare, Medicaid, Tricare for military families,

Veterans Administration (VA) care for veterans, and so on. Economists favor it because these transfers are explicit rather than hidden, and politicians can be held accountable for them.

The second transfer mechanism—community-rated health insurance premiums (of which more further on)—has been a hallmark of Obamacare. As is well known, it has created huge actuarial problems[3] in that context. It also has burdened healthier members of the middle class who are asked to subsidize sicker individuals. More will be said about these problems further on as well.

Apparently unbeknownst to many Americans covered by employment-based insurance, community rating also is baked into that system. Two employees performing the same work for a given company, one healthy and the other one chronically ill, usually make the same contribution out of their paychecks toward their insurance coverage. In other words, healthy employees indirectly subsidize chronically ill employees.

Can we imagine the outcry among employees—especially unionized employees—if a company tried to extract a larger contribution toward health insurance from chronically ill employees than from chronically healthy employees? Or can we imagine how elderly and most likely sicker members of Congress and their staffs would react if their contribution to their health insurance coverage were not community rated but instead based on *actuarially fair* pricing, taking each member's health status into account?

The third transfer mechanism—price discrimination—also is an integral feature of the U.S. health care delivery system. Doctors, hospitals, and other providers of health care routinely engage in it. Clever public relations people can pitch it as an angelic Robin Hood–like mechanism that robs the rich to help the poor. However, that system also can serve as a perfect platform for outright financial rapaciousness, visiting great financial distress on members of the middle class.[4]

3

∎

Some Interesting or Curious Facts about Our Health Care System

Americans pride themselves on being "exceptional." A number of facts about the U.S. health care system are indeed exceptional, and some are downright bizarre or curious.

The Bizarre Nature and Role of Prices in U.S. Health Care

It was noted earlier that U.S. prices for any type of health care service or product tend to be at least twice as high as comparable prices in other developed countries. The data shown in that section were just *average* prices. In fact, there are huge variations in prices about these averages. As the *Yale News*[1] noted in commenting on recent research by Yale health economist Zachary Cooper and colleagues[2] elsewhere, "Hospital prices show 'mind-boggling' variation across U.S., driving up health care costs."

Figure 3.1, taken directly from these authors' paper, illustrates this huge variation in prices.

As figure 3.1 shows, there is no such thing as a "price" a hospital charges or is paid for a particular procedure. What the hospital is paid depends on the payer (Medicaid, Medicare, private insurer, or self-paying patients).

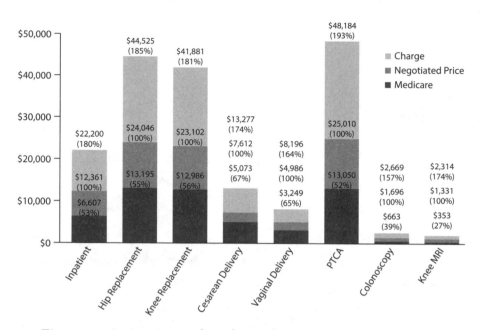

Figure 3.1 Average Hospital Facilities Charges, Negotiated Prices, and Medicare Reimbursements, 2008–2011. The height of the light gray bar (top) is the average hospital charge price. The height of the medium gray bar (middle) is the negotiated (transaction) price, which is regression adjusted. The dark gray bar (bottom) captures the Medicare reimbursement. Note that we only include hospital-based prices—so we exclude, for example, colonoscopies performed in surgical centers and MRIs that are not carried out in hospitals.
Source: Zack Cooper, Stuart V. Craig, Martin Gaynor, and John Van Reenen, *The Quarterly Journal of Economics*, 2018, qjy020, by permission of Oxford University Press.

In addition, even within the private insurance sector, the price of a particular procedure varies widely among insurers for a given hospital, and among hospitals, for a given insurer.

Moreover, even for one hospital, the price of a given procedure paid by a given insurer varies by the type of insurance policy the patient has (for example, Health Maintenance Organization [HMO] or Preferred Provider Organization [PPO]). In a nutshell, total chaos reigns.

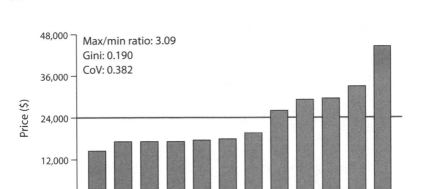

Figure 3.2 Knee Replacement, Denver, CO.

"Charge" in figure 3.1 refers to the list prices each hospital has in its "charge master." These list prices often are so high as to defy reason. Each hospital composes its own charge master, using methods that remain a mystery to outsiders.[3]

The charge masters of different hospitals do not even have a common structure and nomenclature. Only a few state governments have the temerity to require hospitals to post their charge masters on their websites.

However, uninsured patients with some means typically are charged these high list prices. Hospitals then use any means, including debt collectors and the courts, to collect on bills at these high charges. Considerable detail[4] on this practice can be found in journalist Steven Brill's book *The Bitter Pill*[5] and in Elisabeth Rosenthal's 2017 book *An American Sickness.*[6] Medical bills based on charges can easily bankrupt a family.[7]

Usually private health insurers negotiate the prices they will pay hospitals in the form of discounts off the hospital's charge master, although sometimes these negotiations are for prices of particular procedures. These prices are shown as "negotiated prices" in figure 3.1. They are averages, with huge variations within these averages.

Finally, Medicare prices are those paid by Medicare. In principle, they are set to cover the average cost of hospitals, although for some hospitals there is a shortfall of Medicare prices from costs, while for other hospitals Medicare's prices may yield a positive profit margin.

A fascinating feature of U.S. prices for health care is not only that they vary so much across this huge country, but also that they vary just as much within localities, for example, within a city, county, or state.

The authors of the research paper cited above (Cooper et al.) illustrate this with price variations for particular procedures within cities—for example, Denver in figure 3.2.

Earlier, in 2008, as chair of the New Jersey Commission on Rationalizing Health Care Resources, I had asked the CEO of Blue Cross Blue Shield Horizon of New Jersey, the largest health insurer in the state, what his company actually paid for a routine screening colonoscopy (not list prices). The answer was "more than 50 distinct prices, sometimes different prices to the same hospital, depending on the insurance policy of the patient." Similarly, I had asked Wellpoint Inc. (now Anthem) on the West Coast what they actually paid different hospitals in the state for identical standard procedures.

Tables 3.1 and 3.2 show these price differentials for New Jersey and California, respectively. The price variations in these charts are enormous.

Just what drives these huge price variations remains a mystery. There is no empirical evidence showing any correlation between these prices and the quality of health care delivered, nor is there any correlation with production costs.

One could eliminate these variations through what is known among researchers as all-payer systems, with uniform fee schedules applying to all providers and all insurers within a state. Germany, France, Switzerland, and most other developed countries take this approach. However, neither U.S.

Table 3.1 Large New Jersey Insurer's Payment for Colonoscopies
Performed in Hospitals and Ambulatory Surgical Centers

Cost per Colonoscopy	In-Network Minimum to Maximum Range
Physician	$178 to $431
Hospital	$716 to $3,717
ASC	$443 to $1,395

Source: Data from NJ Commission on Rationalizing Health Care Resources, 2008 Final Report.

Table 3.2 Payments by One California Insurer to Various Hospitals, 2007
(Wage Adjusted)

	Appendectomy[a]	CABG[b]
Hospital A	$1,800	$33,000
Hospital B	$2,900	$54,600
Hospital C	$4,700	$64,500
Hospital D	$9,500	$72,300
Hospital E	$13,700	$99,800

[a]Cost per case (DRG 167).
[b]Coronary bypass with cardiac catheterization (DRG 107); tertiary hospitals only.
Source: Data from NJ Commission on Rationalizing Health Care Resources, 2008 Final Report.

providers of health care nor U.S. health insurers nor the U.S. Congress has any appetite for such a simplified approach, which would significantly reduce the administrative overhead of the system. (In this regard, see this author's "The Pricing of Hospital Services: Chaos behind a Veil of Secrecy"[8] and "The Many Different Prices Paid to Providers and the Flawed Theory of Cost Shifting: Is It Time for a More Rational All-Payer System?"[9]) To date, only Maryland has an all-payer system.

The Pervasive Lack of Price Transparency

Part of the debate on health reform in this country has been the idea that patients should be converted from patients to regular consumers with "skin in the game." To that end, patients would be incentivized through high annual deductibles and high coinsurance to shop around smartly for cost-effective health care—health care of high quality, efficiently produced. It is a favorite theory among health economists and certain politicians they inspire, although it is faith-based, resting on data-free analysis.

In a 2015 column[10] entitled "This Study Is Forcing Economists to Rethink High-Deductible Health Insurance," Sarah Kliff of *Vox* cited a study[11] by highly reputable health economists finding that people just do not behave as the theory predicts. Few employees of a large firm actually used the tools their employer provided to shop around for cost-effective health care. High deductibles simply induced them to forego both high-value and low-value health services.

A major problem with the economists' theory of high deductibles is that patients typically do not know binding prices and robust data on the quality of care when they approach the health system. In effect, they enter that market like blindfolded shoppers pushed into a department store, there to shop around smartly for whatever item they might want or, in the case of health care, need. Consequently, implementation of the economists' theory of patients shopping around for cost-effective care so far has been a cruel hoax. It merely has served to push the U.S. health system toward more extensive rationing of health care by income class. If that is what health economists wanted, they should have said so forthrightly.

To be sure, most large health insurance companies now attempt to provide their customers with so-called cost estimators that purport to show differences in the overall cost of particular treatments by doctor or hospital. But these are only rough estimates, not binding prices. Moreover, the physician's or hospital bill patients receive—usually completely incomprehensible to the patient—may deviate significantly from these cost estimates.

Surprise Medical Bills

There is the additional problem that a patient may choose a hospital in his or her insurer's network with negotiated prices, but that, unbeknownst to the patient, the radiologists, anesthesiologists, pathologists, or emergency room physicians working in the hospital may be out-of-network. They then are free to present to patients so-called surprise medical bills[12] not constrained by any negotiated prices.

Insurers in those cases usually will reimburse the patient at what their negotiated price for in-network physicians would have been, leaving the patient to pay out-of-network physicians the difference between those negotiated prices and whatever these physicians chose to charge them.

It is hard to think of a more unfair financial arrangement between patients and the health care system, one in which the buy side is virtually defenseless vis-à-vis the supply side, and it is hard to imagine that any other country would allow it.

A 2016 analysis[13] by Yale researchers found that a U.S. average of 22 percent of emergency room visits entail such out-of-network physicians and their surprise medical bills, although there is a wide variation in this percentage about the average. (For a truly dramatic news story on surprise medical bills, see the *New York Times* article "After Surgery, Surprise $117,000 Medical Bill from Doctor He Didn't Know.")[14]

The American Health Insurance Plans (AHIP), the national organization of private health plans, from time to time publishes data on out-of-network billings. Table 3.3 is taken from their most recent study.

Table 3.3. Summary of Out-of-Network Billed Charges Compared to the 2014 Medicare Physician Fee Schedule

CPT Code*	Description	Event Count	Provider Count	Average Medicare Fee (2014)	Average OON Charge Submitted (2013–2014)	Average Charge as a % of Medicare	OON Billed Charges, 25th Percentile	OON Billed Charges, 75th Percentile	IQR**
62310	Injection spine cervical/thoracic	25,167	4,680	$ 113	$ 1,152	1022.7%	$ 470	$ 1,307	$ 837
63030	Low back disk surgery	4,516	1,514	$ 1,004	$ 9,426	938.5%	$ 3,013	$ 10,216	$ 7,204
63075	Neck spine disk surgery	452	194	$ 1,414	$ 10,459	739.7%	$ 3,289	$ 10,975	$ 7,686
70553	MRI of brain with and without dye	16,404	3,554	$ 405	$ 2,929	723.1%	$ 1,917	$ 3,639	$ 1,722
47562	Laparoscopic cholecystectomy	10,986	3,851	$ 676	$ 4,827	713.8%	$ 1,710	$ 4,930	$ 3,220
15734	Muscle-skin graft trunk	1,485	561	$ 1,547	$ 10,798	698.0%	$ 3,565	$ 14,998	$ 11,433
76942	Ultrasonic guide for biopsy	105,921	11,229	$ 76	$ 517	685.0%	$ 275	$ 600	$ 325
29881	Knee arthroscopy/ surgery	5,395	1,721	$ 561	$ 3,410	607.5%	$ 1,650	$ 3,483	$ 1,833
22612	Lumbar spine fusion	4,946	1,491	$ 1,651	$ 9,884	598.8%	$ 3,800	$ 10,100	$ 6,300
99285	Emergency dept visit high severity	1,157,761	15,784	$ 176	$ 971	551.5%	$ 680	$ 1,255	$ 575

Code	Description								
27130	Total hip arthroplasty	2,879	933	$1,411	$7,491	531.1%	$3,960	$8,073	$4,113
77418	Intensity modulated radiation therapy	84,340	964	$404	$1,734	429.7%	$1,288	$2,029	$741
57288	Repair bladder defect	1,770	983	$742	$2,910	392.2%	$1,562	$3,156	$1,594
19120	Removal of breast lesion	871	604	$503	$1,887	375.1%	$858	$1,809	$951
33533	Coronary artery bypass, single artery	3,734	924	$1,970	$7,329	372.0%	$4,773	$8,342	$3,569
44140	Partial removal of colon	1,143	831	$1,384	$4,951	357.8%	$2,700	$4,500	$1,800
96413	Chemotherapy IV infusion 1 hr	131,554	4,388	$136	$437	321.6%	$300	$573	$273
66984	Cataract surgery with insertion of lens	5,834	1,030	$683	$2,172	318.2%	$1,615	$2,500	$885
88305	Tissue exam by pathologist	757,814	11,807	$72	$227	314.9%	$155	$275	$120
26055	Incise finger tendon sheath	1,536	767	$570	$1,652	290.0%	$899	$1,780	$881
99291	Critical care first hour	295,376	18,243	$279	$795	285.0%	$450	$996	$546

(continued)

Table 3.3. (*continued*)

CPT Code*	Description	Event Count	Provider Count	Average Medicare Fee (2014)	Average OON Charge Submitted (2013–2014)	Average Charge as a % of Medicare	OON Billed Charges, 25th Percentile	OON Billed Charges, 75th Percentile	IQR**
43239	Upper GI endoscopy with biopsy	88,584	12,900	$413	$1,062	257.2%	$579	$1,089	$510
45380	Colonoscopy and biopsy	48,439	10,564	$478	$1,207	252.5%	$800	$1,361	$561
36471	Injection therapy of veins	3,816	521	$181	$446	246.6%	$276	$475	$199
11042	Debridement, subcut tissue ≤20 sq cm	57,580	7,295	$119	$280	235.0%	$137	$300	$163
99233	Subsequent hospital care	1,282,457	49,205	$106	$239	225.3%	$155	$255	$100
97140	Manual therapy ≥1 regions	4,105,566	33,713	$31	$66	215.2%	$44	$81	$37
97110	Therapeutic exercises	9,854,881	48,474	$33	$65	196.7%	$42	$81	$39
17311	Mohs micrographic technique 1st stage	40,317	2,909	$667	$1,199	179.8%	$805	$1,370	$565
99215	Office outpatient visit 40 minutes	817,491	77,628	$147	$260	176.8%	$175	$304	$129

Source: AHIP, Charges Billed by Out-Of-Network Providers: Implications for Affordability, https://www.ahip.org/wp-content/uploads/2015/09/OON_Report_11.3.16.pdf.

*CPT copyright 2014 American Medical Association. All rights reserved. CPT is a registered trademark of the American Medical Association.

**IQR = Interquartile Range; the difference between the 75th percentile and the 25th percentile.

Does Health Care Create or Kill Jobs?

One facet of health care may be of interest to macroeconomists, namely, the *job-creating capacity* of the health sector. It has for many years been the largest job creator in the economy, offering jobs at all skill levels, and noticeably hospitable to women and minorities. Of course, from a microeconomic perspective this job-creating capacity is valuable to society only if it produces output of value to society.

According to a cosmic law whose discovery I attribute to the legendary Harvard professor Alfred E. Neuman:

Every dollar health spending = Someone's health-care income.

It follows that total national health spending must be mirrored in total national health care incomes and employment.

In a study[15] undertaken for the Council on Foreign Relations, Sandile Hlatshwayo and Nobel laureate in economics Michael Spence found the U.S. health sector to be the largest job creator in the entire U.S. economy over the period 1990–2008, as figure 3.3 shows. During that period, the U.S. health sector created six million additional jobs, followed by the government sector with four million new jobs. All other sectors contributed fewer new jobs, even the construction industry, which boomed during those years.

How might recent health reform proposals affect employment in the United States? The answers given by economists depend on their political leanings.

To illustrate, in his "How Many Jobs Does the ACA Kill?,"[16] University of Chicago economist Casey B. Mulligan reports that the regulations the ACA imposed on small business firms killed as many as 250,000 jobs. That finding, however, is neatly offset by another study in April 2017,[17] also by economists, finding that

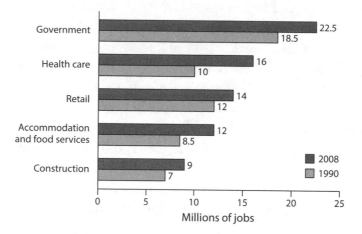

Figure 3.3 Employment in Various Sectors of the U.S. Economy, 1990 and 2008.
Source: Approximated from Spence and Hlatswayo, Figure 6.

the ACA actually created an estimated 240,000 new health care jobs[18] by injecting over a trillion dollars of new health spending over the ensuing decade (5 percent more than would otherwise have been spent).

Much the same collective professional ignorance applied to the Republican health reform proposals of 2017. Both the House and the Senate bills would have withdrawn about $1.1 trillion of federal spending on health care from the health care sector over the next decade. A June 2017 study[19] found that by withdrawing these sums from health care, the American Health Care Act of 2017 (popularly known as Ryancare) that passed the U.S. House of Representatives in May 2017 as H.R. 1628 would be a major job killer in health care.[20] An even larger job loss was imputed to the Senate's draft bill. The opposite conclusions, however, surely could be had from economists of a different ideological persuasion.

Collectively as a profession, economists probably do not have a clue on how many jobs particular health reform proposals create or destroy (see figure 3.4). This is par for the course for an

Figure 3.4
Source: PRICKLY CITY ©2009 Scott Stantis. Dist. By ANDREWS MCMEEL
SYNDICATION. Reprinted with permission. All rights reserved.

academic discipline that is as much ideology practiced in the
guise of science as it is actual science. Economists are at ideological loggerheads on many issues in public policy, including
macroeconomics. Right-wing economists make a solid "scientific" case for tax cuts as a remedy for macroeconomic malaise.
Left-of-center economists make an equally solid "scientific" case
for higher government spending as a cure for macroeconomic
malaise. Thus confused by the "science," politicians vote for whatever approach they and their constituents like best.

The Health System as a Tax System

While to macroeconomists the job-creating capacity of the
health sector is one of its salutary features, the mirror image of
that feature is the enormous fiscal burden the sector imposes on
the rest of society.

Given the often clinically and morally compelling nature of
health care as a commodity, one can think of a nation's health
system as just another tax system, operating side by side with the
government's tax system.

For the most part, however, citizens have far fewer defenses against that health care "tax" than they have against the government's tax system, other than foregoing even clinically needed health care through self-rationing. Government tax rates are known in advance. Furthermore, there are numerous legal maneuvers to evade taxes owed the government.

By contrast, prices for health care typically are not known to patients ahead of treatment, nor do most patients have the technical know-how to judge the merits and quality of the care they receive (not really "demand"). As Austin Frakt reports in "The Puzzling Popularity of Spine Surgery in Certain Regions,"[21] rates of certain medical treatments—for example, spine surgery or cardiac treatments—vary enormously and inexplicably among localities in the United States. It takes a hard-core economist, beholden to faith-based theories, to believe that these variations reflect demand by patients, forged by their knowledge about the appropriate care for their medical conditions. Much more probably these variations reflect the belief among physicians of what is the appropriate care or the financial incentives physicians face to favor one treatment over another.

Therefore, medical bills issued by doctors, hospitals, and other providers of health care after treatment typically are surprises—often very unpleasant surprises, especially because most medical bills are incomprehensible to patients, probably deliberately so (see figure 3.5). There can be profit in obfuscation.

Most prices for health care in the United States are kept as trade secrets between insurers and providers of care. The only exceptions are said to occur in the markets for LASIK and cosmetic surgery, where physicians usually do apprise patients of prices ahead of the treatment.

As noted earlier, the health care "tax" system takes a haircut of 18 percent of GDP. It is projected to take 20 percent by 2025. These numbers, however, actually understate the burden of the health care "tax" on American households. Ideally, we should

Figure 3.5

relate total national health spending not to GDP but to total *personal national income,* because all health spending is extracted from the personal national income of private households, not from GDP.

The Federal Reserve Bank of St. Louis provides a neat explanation[22] of the difference between GDP and *personal income.* To arrive at personal income, one must deduct from GDP an estimate of the wear and tear (depreciation) of capital equipment (known in the national income accounts as "capital consumption allowance"). There are also a number of other items—for example, income retained by corporations—that must be deducted from GDP to arrive at personal income. On average, the latter is about 86 percent of GDP.

Therefore, an 18 percent claim of health care on GDP in 2016 actually represents a 21 percent "tax" on personal income. The projected 20 percent of GDP by 2025 actually represents a 23 percent claim on total personal income in the United States—almost a quarter.

By comparison, total taxes of any type, at all levels of government in the United States, amounted to 26.4 percent of GDP in 2015, or 30 percent of personal income—by the way, one of the *lowest* tax-to-GDP ratios in the OECD.[23] Therefore, as a tax system, the health system is not quite as burdensome as general government taxation, but it is a close rival in the United States.

4

■

Who Actually Pays for Health Care?

Logically, it must be true that all spending on the health system in any country originates 100 percent from the budgets of private households. That fact is not fully appreciated by the general public when it argues, for example, that "government should pay for health care for the poor." This is only vaguely correct, as should be evident from figure 4.1.

Government-run health insurance programs (e.g., traditional Medicare) write the final checks to the providers of health care for patients covered by these programs; but government obtains the cash for these payments by sucking money out of household budgets via taxes.

Similarly, private employers write the checks to private insurers to cover the premiums for employees, and the latter then pay doctors, hospitals, and other providers of health care; but private employers recoup these outlays by reducing their employees' take-home pay or trimming their other fringe benefits (e.g., pensions).

Finally, private insurers selling policies in the individual market for health insurance directly suck money out of household budgets in the form of premiums.

None of these final-check writers actually pays a single dime for health care. They all recover their outlays from the budgets of private households.

Figure 4.2 shows the decomposition of U.S. health spending in 2015 by final payer, that is, the payer who writes the final check to the providers of health care.

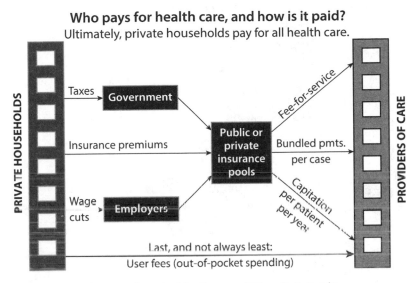

Who pays for health care, and how is it paid?
Ultimately, private households pay for all health care.

Figure 4.1 Who Pays for Health Care, and How Is It Paid?

The Role of Public Health Insurance

Often not appreciated by the public is that roughly half of all U.S. health spending now runs directly through government budgets: Medicare, Medicaid, Tricare for the military, VA care, and public health. Thus, on the financing side, the U.S. health system long ago ceased to be a mainly private system. Two ironies may be noted in passing.

Irony 1: Is a Single-Payer Health Insurance System Un-American?

It is often argued that a single-payer health care system, such as those of the Canadian provinces or of Taiwan and Korea, is unthinkable for the United States.[1]

Is that actually true? It is not.

The still widely popular[2] public Medicare system for America's elderly and those afflicted with disabilities and renal failure,

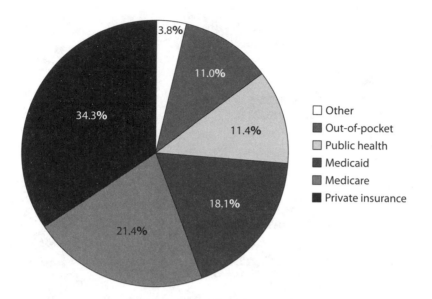

Figure 4.2 U.S. Spending on Health Care by Final Payer, 2015.
Source: "National Health Expenditure Projections, 2015–25: Economy, Prices, and Aging Expected to Shape Spending and Enrollment." Sean P. Keehan, John A. Poisal, Gigi A. Cuckler, Andrea M. Sisko, Sheila D. Smith, Andrew J. Madison, Devin A. Stone, Christian J. Wolfe, and Joseph M. Lizonitz. *Health Affairs* 2016 35:8, 1522–1531.

passed in 1965, is a *classic single-payer system*, run by the central (federal) government of this huge and varied country, with uniform fee schedules and rules applicable everywhere in the land. Even Canada's health system is not that centralized, as each province operates its own single-payer system.

To be sure, elderly Americans now have a choice to remain with the traditional government-run single-payer system or to opt out in favor of identical and often more extensive coverage by private health insurers—the so-called Medicare Advantage program enacted in 2003 with that year's H.R. 1, the Medicare Prescription Drug, Improvement, and Modernization Act of 2003.[3] Much is made of the fact that by now some 30 percent of Medicare beneficiaries have opted for private insurers under the Medicare Advantage program. More amazing, however, is that even after more than a decade (since 2003), some 70 percent of Medicare beneficiaries still choose to remain with the traditional government-run single-payer system.

It is interesting to speculate why this might be so, as I did in a column in the *Journal of the American Medical Association* (*JAMA*).[4] My hypothesis is that Medicare beneficiaries value highly the freedom of choice of doctor and hospital that the traditional government-run single-payer Medicare program still offers them, while in private Medicare Advantage plans they typically find their choice of doctors and other providers of health care limited to often narrow networks of these providers.

Irony 2: Is Purely Socialized Medicine *Un-American?*

A second irony lies in this nation's almost instinctive loathing of "socialized medicine." Do we actually loathe it? The answer appears to be no once again.

For starters, we must distinguish here between "social insurance" and "socialized medicine." They are not the same.

Canada, Germany, Switzerland, Taiwan, Korea, and Japan operate *social health insurance* systems, but the *health care delivery system* is a mixture of public and private institutions, including for-profit institutions. These nations' health systems do not represent "socialized medicine."

Under "socialized medicine," not only is the health insurance system socialized (under government control), but government also owns and operates all the health care production facilities. The original National Health Service (NHS) of Great Britain was purely socialized medicine, as is, for example, the system run by the Hong Kong Hospital Authority.

In the United States, we reserve a purely *socialized medicine* system for Americans we claim to thank and adore: our military veterans. Under the VA health system, the government not only owns and controls the financing of health care, but it also owns and operates all health care production facilities.[5] It is fair to ask why, if *socialized medicine* is so bad, Americans for almost a century now have preserved precisely that construct for their military veterans, and, indeed, why the latter are so defensive and protective of that socialized medicine system. It is a remarkable irony.

Are Medicare and Medicaid Unsustainable?

A canard frequently heard in the debate on health reform is that Medicare and Medicaid are the main cost drivers in U.S. health care and are, in fact, "unsustainable." That question has been addressed in the Introduction of this book and therefore I will not repeat that discussion here, other than to reiterate that such an argument is a highly dubious argument.

If I had to pick a locomotive for health spending in America, I would point to employment-based health insurance. Economists are convinced, by theory and empirical research, that employers typically recoup their contribution to their employees' health insurance from the employees through cuts in take-home pay or other fringe benefits. As a research paper in *Health Affairs*, entitled "A Decade of Health Care Growth Has Wiped Out Real Income Gains for an Average U.S. Family"[6] concluded:

> Although a median-income US family of four with employer-based health insurance saw its gross annual income increase from $76,000 in 1999 to $99,000 in 2009, this gain was largely offset by increased spending to pay for health care.

Presumably, employers know that they can shift back their contribution to their employees' health insurance into the employees' paychecks. On the other hand, employees may believe that "the company" pays for the bulk of their health care cost. Therefore, in an inflationary pas de deux, neither party has had a strong incentive over the years to control their spending on health care. The huge public subsidies employment-based health insurance receives from the government further enhance this inflationary tendency.

The Huge Public Subsidy to Employment-Based Private Health Insurance

It is a little-known fact that employed Americans covered by employer-sponsored health insurance receive a generous public subsidy toward their coverage, a subsidy whose generosity rises with the income of the employee.

Although employer-sponsored health insurance relies exclusively on private health insurance carriers, it is the beneficiary of a significant *tax preference*. Employers can deduct their contribution to their employees' health insurance as a business expense. Although that contribution clearly is part of the employees' compensation, it is not taxable compensation to employees, as are wages and salary. Furthermore, employee benefit managers can make the employees' own contribution also come out of pretax income. The higher the income and thus the marginal tax rate faced by an employee, the more he or she benefits from this tax preference.[7]

Naturally, the beneficiaries of this huge public subsidy have made it politically impossible to rid the system of this regressive subsidy, and Congress has always gone along with it. The sanctity of that much-cherished public subsidy has long been the third rail of the politics of health reform.

Employed Americans—especially high-income employees—who may have misgivings over the federal subsidies paid low-income Americans under Obamacare may be surprised to learn

that the federal subsidies they are given through the tax preference granted employment-based health insurance are estimated
to total $250 billion[8] a year—closer to $300 billion if foregone
state tax revenues are included. That subsidy is about two and a
half to three times the total public subsidies paid low-income
Americans under Obamacare, which in 2016 cost the federal
government only $110 billion and the states basically nothing.[9]

To economists, there is something comical about Americans
wringing their hands over the nation's entitlement spending, all
the while having their paws so squarely in the public trough.

5

■

Value for the Money Spent on
U.S. Health Care

Compared to other developed nations, do Americans receive commensurately higher value for their high spending on health care? Although it is very difficult to answer that question, the available empirical research suggests that Americans are short changed on that score.

Earlier I argued that one could think of our health system as a giant tax system, like the government's regular tax system.

A government tax system is not just a sinkhole into which money disappears without yielding the citizenry value in return. Government provides many highly valuable services that are the very foundation of economic development and growth in the private sector: external and internal security, administration of a body of law, provision of education, physical infrastructure, highly valuable R&D, and so on.

Similarly, the health system is a "tax" system that returns to citizens highly valuable services, including lifesaving treatments. Even so, it is fair to ask whether, for all the "taxes" Americans do pay to their health system—on average now 21 percent of their personal income—they get commensurately higher value than do citizens in countries that spend less.

The answer is mixed.

On the one hand, the U.S. health care delivery system offers patients able to pay for their health care—through insurance or out-of-pocket spending—an abundance of sophisticated health care services and products, often delivered in relatively luxurious settings, on a timely basis, without the queuing one sometimes observes in other developed countries, notably in Canada and the UK.

On the other hand, however, cross-national surveys[1] show that a higher proportion of Americans than people in other developed nations deny themselves access to needed health care over out-of-pocket costs or have serious problems paying their medical bills.[2] There are still some twenty million uninsured Americans, and even those who do have health insurance increasingly face ever-higher deductibles and coinsurance.

Figure 5.1[3] illustrates this point. This self-rationing by American patients could have a negative impact[4] on their health status.

Health Status Indicators

Presumably the objective of a health system is to help maintain or improve the physical and mental health status of individuals and, thus, of populations. Ideally, then, one should evaluate the performance of health systems by their impact on *health status metrics*—for example, infant mortality rates and maternal death rates, life expectancy at birth or other specified ages (for example, age sixty-five), or cancer survival rates.

The problem, of course, is that these metrics are impacted not only by health care, but also by many environmental, socioeconomic, and behavioral factors not under the control of the health system. Indeed, while for individuals timely and appropriate health care can be a matter of life or death, for population-based metrics, health care proper has generally been

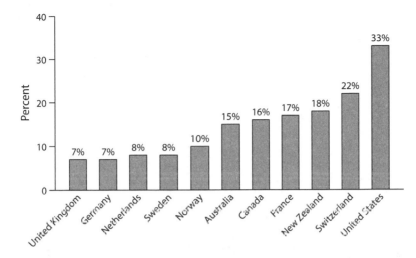

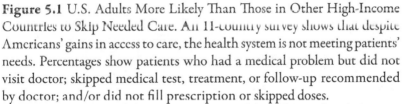

Figure 5.1 U.S. Adults More Likely Than Those in Other High-Income Countries to Skip Needed Care. An 11-country survey shows that despite Americans' gains in access to care, the health system is not meeting patients' needs. Percentages show patients who had a medical problem but did not visit doctor; skipped medical test, treatment, or follow-up recommended by doctor; and/or did not fill prescription or skipped doses.
Source: "In New Survey of Eleven Countries, US Adults Still Struggle with Access to and Affordability of Health Care." Robin Osborn, David Squires, Michelle M. Doty, Dana O. Sarnak, and Eric C. Schneider. *Health Affairs* 2016 35:12, 2327–2336.

found[5] to contribute no more than 10 percent to 20 percent of observed cross-country variations in these metrics.

To illustrate this important point—so often overlooked by critics of U.S. health care—it is illuminating to examine the prevalence of obesity by country and the evident correlation between obesity rates and the prevalence of diabetes.

Figure 5.2 does not show obesity rates for the UK (26.9 percent in 2015) and for New Zealand (30.7 percent in 2015). They are high up the obesity scale. I have no explanation for the fact that the prevalence of obesity seems to be particularly high in English-speaking countries. (Could it be that speaking English makes you fat?)

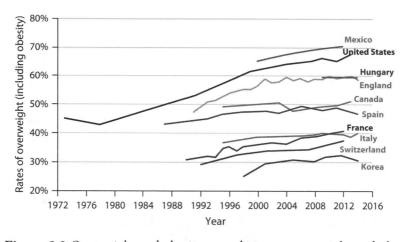

Figure 5.2 Overweight and obesity rates designate overweight and obesity prevalence rates. Age- and gender-adjusted rates of overweight (including obesity), using the 2005 OECD standard population. Measured height and weight in England, Hungary, Korea, Mexico, and the United States; self-reported in other countries.
Source: OECD (2017), Obesity Update 2017, available at http://www.oecd.org/els/health-systems/Obesity-Update-2017.pdf.

The U.S. Centers for Disease Control and Prevention (CDC) has for years tracked the prevalence of obesity and diabetes. It has made the data available in easily readable maps,[6] an example of which is reproduced in figure 5.3.

Although physicians are supposed to be, in part, management consultants who help their patients manage their own health more effectively and efficiently, it would be a stretch to blame the growing prevalence of obesity and diabetes in this country on physicians or other parts of the health system. Yet the effect of these trends do reflect themselves in measurable health status indicators.

With that caveat, I present some data that may possibly be impacted by health care, although it is hard to know to what extent. Figure 5.4 comes from a neat new website, the "health

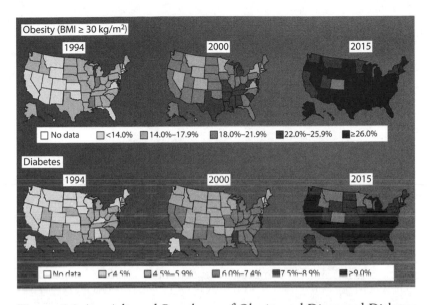

Figure 5.3 Age-Adjusted Prevalence of Obesity and Diagnosed Diabetes among U.S. Adults.
Source: CDC's Division of Diabetes Translation, http://www.cdc.gov/diabetes/data.

systems tracker"[7] operated jointly by the Peterson Institute and the Kaiser Family Foundation.

Evidently, on this metric the United States does not score well at any time and over time. Although often mentioned in indictments of the U.S. health system—see, for example, the Institute of Medicine's study "U.S. Health in International Perspective: Shorter Lives, Poorer Health"[8]—life expectancy is a treacherous metric. First, life expectancy at birth is nothing other than the sum of guestimated future age-specific survival probabilities, all the way from age 0 to age 100.[9] As any demographer will admit, projecting these future survival probabilities is really a guessing game. Second, whatever these survival probabilities may be, they are driven by many factors other than health care proper.

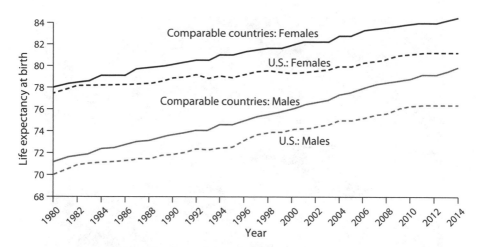

Figure 5.4 Life Expectancy at Birth, 1980–2014.
Source: Peterson-Kaiser Health System Tracker, https://www.healthsystemtracker.org
/indicator/health-well-being/life-expectancy/.

Table 5.1 shows five-year cancer survival rates for particular types of cancer and some relevant countries with which the United States can fairly be compared. The bold, enlarged numbers in a column denote the highest five-year survival rate for that column. On that metric, the United States generally does rather well, although not for all types of cancer.

Comparative studies of cancer mortality or survival rates remain controversial as well, for at least two reasons.

First, if the comparison is based simply on mortality rates, it runs into the problem that many factors other than health care drive that mortality. Of interest, however, is the marginal impact of health care on these rates, other things being equal.

Researchers try to avoid this trap by focusing instead on X-year survival after diagnosis. Presumably, once an illness is diagnosed, its future course will be more powerfully driven by health care. But here, too, it is sometimes objected that this metric may

Table 5.1 Five-Year Survival Rates for Patients Diagnosed with Five Common Cancers in Seven Countries, 2005–2009

Country	Female Breast	Colon	Lung	Prostate	Childhood Leukemia
Canada*	85.8	62.8	17.3	91.7	90.6
France**	86.9	59.8	13.6	90.5	89.2
Germany	85.3	64.6	16.2	91.2	**91.8**
Italy	86.2	63.2	14.7	89.7	87.7
Japan	84.7	64.4	**30.1**	86.8	81.1
United Kingdom*	81.1	53.8	9.6	83.2	89.1
United States	**88.6**	**64.7**	18.7	**97.2**	87.7

Source: "Cancer Survival: The Start of Global Surveillance," 2015 CDC, https://www.cdc.gov/cancer/dcpc/research/articles/concord-2.htm.
*Countries with 100% population coverage.
**100% population coverage for children only.

measure more the timing of the diagnosis, rather than the impact of health care on survival. One could imagine a type of cancer that is simply not responsive to medical treatment. Then, if one country tends to diagnose that cancer earlier than another country, the first would spuriously rank higher on X-year cancer survival rates.

Yet another widely used but still controversial metric in cross-national comparisons is the so-called mortality amenable to health care.[10] It refers to mortality that could have been avoided through timely and appropriate health care. The OECD regularly gathers data on this metric and publishes it in its database.

On that metric, the United States does not rank well[11] either (see figure 5.5).

The same conclusion emerged from the previously cited study of the Institute of Medicine (now National Academy of Medicine) of the National Academies, "U.S. Health in International Perspective: Shorter Lives, Poorer Health."[12]

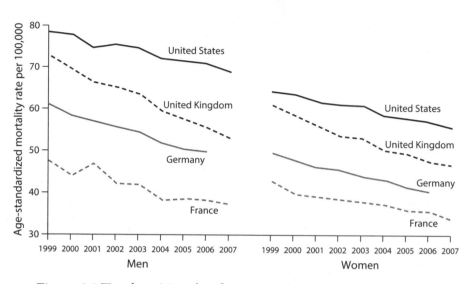

Figure 5.5 Trends in Mortality from Amenable Causes in Four Countries for People under Age 65, 1999–2006/2007.
Source: Author's calculations based on data from the World Health Organization mortality database and Centers for Disease Control and Prevention vital statistics data. Data for Germany for 2007 were not available.

Waste in the U.S. Health System

In addition to rationing many low-income Americans out of health care they believe they need, and possibly contributing to a relatively high mortality rate amenable to health care, there is evidence that the U.S. health system also wastes resources.

In its study *Best Value at Lowest Cost: The Path to Continuously Learning Health Care in America* (2013), for example, the Institute of Medicine presented the following table (table 5.2). The experts on the study panel concluded that close to a third of all health spending in the United States represents waste. A number of highly respected health economists[13] accept[14] these estimates.

Table 5.2 Sources of Estimated Excess Costs, United States, 2009. Thirty-one percent of total health spending of $2.5 trillion

1. Unnecessary services	$210 billion
2. Inefficiently delivered care	$130 billion
3. Excess administrative costs	$190 billion
4. Excessively high prices	$105 billion
4. Missed prevention opportunities	$ 55 billion
4. Fraud	$ 75 billion
TOTAL	$ 765 billion

Source: Institute of Medicine, *Best Care at Lower Cost* (2013), Table 3-1.

Overall Assessment on "Value for the Money"

Not surprisingly, in view of these data on waste, the U.S. Business Roundtable concluded in its 2009 *Business Roundtable Health Care Value Comparability Study* that on

> a new measure of the "value" (cost and performance) of the U.S. health care system relative to our competitors' systems on a weighted scale, the workers and employers of the United States face a 23 percent "value gap" relative to five leading economic competitors—Canada, Japan, Germany, the United Kingdom and France (the "G-5 group")—and a 46 percent "value gap" compared with emerging competitors Brazil, India and China ("the BIC group").[15]

Coming from this group after a highly sophisticated study, abetted by a group of prominent health economists that included the late Nobel laureate Kenneth Arrow, one must take this conclusion seriously.

II

■

Ethical Perspectives on
U.S. Health Care

6

■

The Social Role of Health Care

Although health care has features of ordinary commodities—it is, after all, bought and sold in the economy—the distributive ethics most nations seek to impose on their health systems set it starkly apart from other commodities.

Health reformers in Europe, Canada, or, say, Taiwan (which operates a government-run single-payer system) usually begin their debates on health reform by making explicit the ethical principles that should constrain health policy.

In Germany, for example, policy makers frequently recite the principle of social solidarity. Canada's Royal Commission report on the future of Canadian health care (2002) is entitled *Building on Values: The Future of Health Care in Canada*,[1] and explicitly states what those ethical values are.

Practically, it means that in Germany 90 percent or so of the population share one egalitarian *statutory health insurance* (SHI) system, while 10 percent or so of high-income individuals and civil servants[2] (including professors) purchase private health insurance. In other European systems, 5 percent to 10 percent of the population also are covered by private health insurance. Private insurance in Canada covers only supplementary insurance (for dental care and prescription drugs); it is not comprehensive insurance. Canadians with means, however, can pay out of pocket to avail themselves of timelier U.S. health care or the more heroic procedures not covered in Canada.

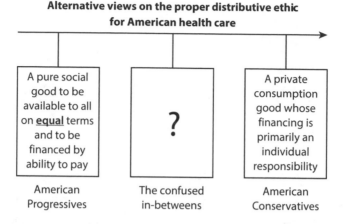

Figure 6.1 Alternative Views on the Proper Distributive Ethic for American Health Care.

For reasons that escape me, Americans typically shy away from an explicit statement on social ethics in debating health reform. Instead, that debate is couched mainly in terms of technical parameters—*actuarially fair versus community-rated* premiums, deductibles, coinsurance, maximum risk exposure, high-risk pools, and so on.

At the risk of oversimplifying, from health reform proposals offered in the United States over the past few decades one can infer two quite distinct ethical principles for the distribution of our nation's health care, as depicted in figure 6.1.

Canada and virtually all European and Asian developed nations have reached, decades ago, a political consensus to treat health care as a *social good*, even though, as already noted, there always is a small upper tier (usually less than 10 percent of the population) that tries to seek care of imagined superior quality through private health insurance.[3]

By contrast, we in the United States have never reached a politically dominant consensus on the issue. We debate these ethical issues only in camouflaged form. The debate in recent years on repealing and replacing Obamacare is merely a continuation of this camouflaged and confusing debate. However, one can infer from actual health reform plans the ethical platform on which they rest.

At the risk, once again, of simplifying too much, it strikes me as fair to say that in the United States, health reform proposals put forth by Democrats tend to lean toward the "social good" vision of health care, although that vision has never been realized. Republican reform proposals tend to treat health care as a private consumption good whose quantity and quality, beyond a bare-bones level, can be rationed by price and willingness to pay, which for most patients probably means "ability" to pay. That vision, too, has never been fully realized.

Further on in this book—in chapters 9 and 10—I will describe and compare the actual reform before the nation (as of fall 2017, the time of this writing) Obamacare, the bill passed by the House as H.R. 1628, the American Health Care Act (AHCA), and the Senate's draft bill H.R. 1628, the Better Care Reconciliation Act (BCRA).

There are two methods by which more direct information on the distributive social ethics could be elicited from the designers of health reform proposals.

One would be to construct a set of scenarios of American families of different sizes, income levels, location, and health status, and then to describe the impact of particular health reform proposals on those families' likely health insurance status, budget, and access to health care. The Congressional Budget Office[4] moves in that direction in its analyses of health reform proposals, but its scenarios are quite limited. Ideally, there should be an interactive website allowing voters to enter their family's particulars, which then yields side-by-side comparisons of the impact of rival health reform proposals. The interactive maps[5] published by the Kaiser Family Foundation come close to that approach.

An alternative approach might be to ask health reformers to indicate, for each family in a sizeable set of alternative scenarios, what fraction of the family's disposable income (or in dollar terms) the family should be required to contribute to health care in the form of its contribution to the premiums for its health insurance and out-of-pocket spending for health care. That would be an illuminating first step in the design of any health reform proposal. It also, of course, would be an efficient way to communicate with voters.

7

∎

The Mechanics of Commercial Health Insurance from an Ethical Perspective

As noted earlier, private health insurance in the United States, as the final payer that pays doctors, hospitals, and other providers of health care, is responsible for about one-third of the total health spending in the United States. Insurers collect premiums from their policy holders to write checks to doctors, hospitals, and other providers of health care.

The pricing of health insurance through premiums can take two quite distinct forms:

a. *medically underwritten (actuarially fair)* health insurance premiums based on the individual applicant's health status, and
b. *community-rated premiums* that are the same for all individuals in large risk pools composed of chronically healthy and chronically sick members.

This chapter explains the differences among these pricing approaches with a simple, stylized numerical example, emphasizing the problems that can arise when community-rated premiums are not supported by a strictly enforced mandate on everyone—young and old—to be insured. That problem has bedeviled the Affordable Care Act of 2010 (Obamacare).

The High Concentration of U.S. Health Spending

Well known to any health policy expert, but perhaps not to the laity, is that in any given year health care spending is concentrated among a few very sick individuals. Figure 7.1 illustrates this phenomenon for the year 2014.

Half the U.S. population did not use much health care at all in 2014. About 90 percent of the population accounted for only 35 percent of all health spending. The most expensive 10 percent of the population accounted for about two-thirds of all health spending, and the most expensive 1 percent for almost 22 percent of all health spending.

This high concentration of health spending among a few individuals is observed for any large group of healthy and sick individuals—for example, employees of large business firms, or large groups of people with mixed health status in any country. Actuaries refer to this as the "80-20" Rule, because typically for any large group of healthy and less healthy people, 20 percent of that group account for roughly 80 percent of that group's health spending.

This concentration curve is roughly the same every year, although U.S. health spending has become slightly more concentrated over the past four decades or so.

Individuals in the upper, most expensive segment of this concentration curve fall into several distinct groups:

1. At one extreme are healthy individuals who met with bad luck during the year because of unforeseen trauma or severe illness.

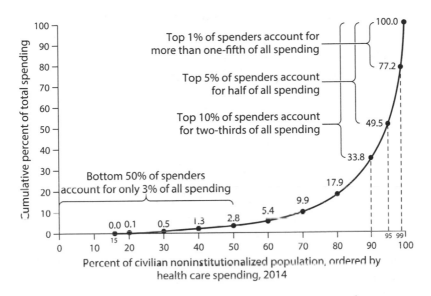

Figure 7.1 Health Care Spending Is Highly Concentrated Among a Small Portion of the U.S. Non-Institutionalized Population.
Source: National Institute for Health Care Management Foundation (NIHCM) analysis of data from the 2013 Medical Expenditure Panel Survey, reprinted with permission.

2. At the other extreme are chronically ill individuals, usually with multiple chronic conditions, who require sustained, expensive medical treatment, typically involving ever more expensive drug therapy.
3. In between are individuals not in perfect health, with various degrees of chronic illness.

Pricing Health Insurance in Unregulated Commercial Markets

Based on the medical histories submitted to them, insurance actuaries usually can accurately classify individuals into distinct risk groups.

A distinct risk group is defined as one all of whose members have, *ex ante*, the same probability distribution of likely future medical expenditures. Another way of saying this is that each member has the same probability of incurring a particular medical expense.

For a large enough membership in the group—more than 20,000 or so—actuaries can then calculate the *probability-weighted average* (also called the *actuarial average* or the *mathematical expectation*) of the risk group's expected per capita medical expenses in the next period (year). Once again, *ex post*, within such a risk pool, most members will be lucky and have no or only very low actual medical expenses. Only a few unlucky ones will have high expenses. *Ex post*, the lucky members of the pool will help finance the health care used by the unlucky ones through the premium they had paid at the beginning of the insurance period. Most economists do not view this as income redistribution, but as the central idea of all forms of insurance.

If an insurer collects from every member of a distinct risk class a premium equal to the probability-weighted expected average medical expense—the *actuarial average* cost for that risk pool—then the total sum collected should be precisely enough to cover all medical expenses of all members of the pool. The technical jargon for such a premium is *actuarially fair*.

To that *actuarially fair* premium the insurer will then add a *load factor* (think of it as a percentage markup) to cover the cost of marketing and administration and to yield a profit margin. The actuarially fair premium plus the load factor then constitute the premium charged the insured.

The natural instinct of commercial insurers is to price health insurance this way. Because the *probability-weighted expected average medical expenses* for risk pools with sicker people are higher than those for pools of healthy people, the premiums charged chronically sicker people naturally will be higher than

Table 7.1 A Simple Stylized Numerical Illustration of the Pricing Strategy of Commercial Health Insurance

Size of medical bill	Fraction of Risk Pool A expected to incur such a medical bill	Fraction of Risk Pool B expected to incur such a medical bill	Fraction of Merged Risk Pools A and B expected to incur such a medical bill
$0	0.85	0.55	0.700
$5,000	0.11	0.36	0.235
$30,000	0.03	0.06	0.045
$100,000	0.01	0.03	0.020
Probability-weighted Average	**$2,450**	**$6,600**	**$4,525**

those charged healthier people. A simple, highly stylized numerical example can illustrate this pricing strategy.

"Actuarially Fair" vs. "Community-Rated" Premiums

Imagine, then, that future health spending could take on only four levels: $0, $5,000, $30,000, and $100,000, as shown in table 7.1.

Assume that in any coming year, people will experience only one of the four medical expenditure levels in the table. The probability of falling into a particular expenditure level, however, varies by risk pool. Table 7.1 shows only two distinct pure risk pools, A and B. Individuals in Pool A are relatively healthy and have a high probability of falling into low expenditure levels. Individuals in Pool B are less healthy. They have a high probability of falling into higher expenditure levels.

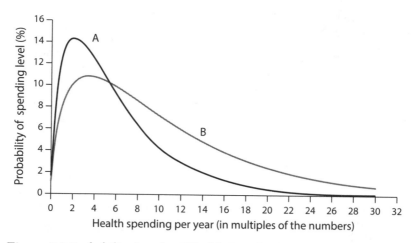

Figure 7.2 Probability Levels of Health Spending Per Capita at Different Levels of Chronic Illness.

In real life, there would of course be myriad different expenditure levels, and each risk group would be characterized by a *probability curve*, such as those shown in figure 7.2.

As already noted, actuaries can accurately predict the probability-weighted average level of spending of particular risk groups exceeding 20,000 members. The relevant *actuarial averages* for each risk group shown are seen in the bottom row of table 7.1.

In a competitive but otherwise unregulated health insurance market, an insurer would assess from the medical histories submitted by applicants for insurance into which risk pool, A or B, individual applicants fall. Applicants falling into Pool A would then be charged a premium equal to

$$\text{Premium}_A = (1+L)\,(\text{probability-weighted average spending of Pool A})$$
$$= (1+L)\,\$2,400, \hspace{3cm} [1]$$

where L is a loading factor to cover marketing, administration, and profits.[1]

Similarly, the insurer would charge each member of Pool B a premium equal to

$$\text{Premium}_B = (1 + L)\ \$6{,}600. \qquad [2]$$

That premium is much higher than the premium for Pool A because, on average, members of Pool B are sicker and more expensive to the insurer than those in Pool A.

Premiums that are based on the health status of the individual applicant are also called *medically underwritten* premiums. The term means that these premiums are based on detailed medical histories that applicants for health insurance must submit to the insurer to allow the latter to price health insurance *actuarially fairly*.

This approach to pricing health insurance obviously represents a deep intrusion by perfect strangers in a distant insurance company into very private, personal matters. With data files of even large companies so vulnerable to hacking, it is a daunting prospect.

Medical underwriting also raises the administrative cost of such a system. In fact, prior to passage of the Affordable Care Act of 2010, health insurance policies sold in the nongroup market were *medically underwritten*. Not surprisingly, because actuaries had to pore over each applicant's medical history, up to 45 percent or so[2] of the premiums charged individuals were devoted by insurers to marketing, administration, and profits, leaving only slightly more than half of the premium to purchase actual health care for the insured. It is amazing that anyone thought this a good bargain.

Although *medically underwritten* insurance premiums make sense to actuaries, economists, and commercial insurance executives, they typically are decried by members of the general public who consider it unfair to charge sicker people higher health insurance premiums. Within the present stylized example, there would be populist political pressure to merge members of Groups A and B into one joint risk pool (the "community") and to price health insurance for each member of that joint group as

$$\text{Premium}_{A+B} = (1 + L)\ \$4{,}525. \qquad [3]$$

Such a premium is defined as *community rated* over the wider risk pool of chronically healthy and chronically sick individuals (the "community"). The Affordable Care Act of 2010 mandated such an approach to insurance pricing for all insurers selling policies in the small-group and nongroup insurance markets. ("Non-group" here means the market in which Americans as individuals purchase health insurance coverage.)

With *community-rated* premiums, members of the healthy Group A would pay a much higher premium than they would under *actuarially fair* pricing. On the other hand, members of the sicker Group B would pay a lower premium than under *actuarially fair* pricing.

In other words, community-rated premiums force ***ex ante*** a redistribution of income from relatively healthier to relatively sicker individuals in the risk pool. As we have learned with Obamacare, that redistribution can rankle the healthier people.

Are Community-Rated Premiums Fair?

A policy question now being hotly debated is whether the income redistribution from healthy to sick Americans that is forced by *community-rated* health insurance premiums is fair. Should community rating be abandoned in favor of *medically underwritten* (*actuarially fair*) premiums, which are higher for sick individuals than for healthier individuals?

Before examining this question in the American context, we should note that most of the world regards *community-rated* health insurance premiums as ethically defensible, that is, as "fair."

1. It is so, for example, in the first national health insurance model, Germany's Bismarckian model, introduced by German chancellor Otto von Bismarck in 1883 as a preemptive strike against the socialist stirrings of the day.
2. It is so in all of the national health systems that have adopted slightly modified versions of the Bismarckian model—for example, the Swiss, French, Belgian, and Dutch systems, the Japanese system, and most of the Latin American systems.
3. The Medicare Advantage program, under which Medicare beneficiaries may choose to obtain insurance coverage from private insurers, also uses community-rated premiums.
4. Finally, as noted earlier, the U.S. employment-based health insurance system uses community-rated premiums, so far without much opposition from younger and healthier employees. It has prompted one commentator to ask wryly in her column, "Where is the outrage over employment-based coverage in the 'rate shock' debate [triggered by Obamacare]?":

   > When it comes to complaints about redistribution and overly-generous benefits in health insurance, why is the echo chamber limited to the individual market? Where is the outrage over employer-sponsored insurance?[3]

5. In fact, actuarially fair (medically underwritten) premiums in the United States were typical only in the small sliver of the health insurance market for individually purchased health insurance (about seven million insured), until Obamacare imposed community-rated premiums on that small market segment as well, to give people in the non-group

market the same community rating Americans have under employment-based coverage.

Some Americans, however, including some legislators, do consider community-rated premiums unfair, even though most of them, if older, actually benefit from them. In an interview on MSNBC, for example, Congressman Mo Brooks (R-AL) argued that people who stay healthy deserve to pay lower premiums for their health insurance. In his words:

> My understanding is that it [the Republican health-reform plan] will allow insurance companies to require people who have higher health care costs to contribute more to the insurance pool that helps offset all these costs, thereby reducing the costs to those people who lead good lives, they're healthy, they've done the things to keep their bodies healthy.

Similarly, when asked whether he agreed with late-night talk show host Jimmy Kimmel that every family, rich or poor, should have access to the kind of excellent care Mr. Kimmel's child received after being born with a congenital heart defect, Mick Mulvaney, President Trump's director of the Office of Management and Budget, responded:

> I do think it [the Republican health reform bill] should meet that test. We have plenty of money to deal with that. We have plenty of money to provide that safety net so that if you get cancer you don't end up broke . . . that is not the question. . . . That doesn't mean we should take care of the person who sits at home, eats poorly and gets diabetes. Is that the same thing as Jimmy Kimmel's kid? I don't think that it is.[4]

This ethical perspective is based on the theory that lifestyle is a major determinant of health status, although clinical scientists constantly remind us that genetic factors, environmental factors, and in utero experiences as fetuses also play important roles in driving the health status of adults.

Part of the debate on social policy in this country has long been the issue of *personal responsibility* versus *social responsibility* for the plight of the nation's vulnerable populations. Conservatives hold that much of that plight can be traced to personal irresponsibility. Progressives on the left argue that vulnerable people are the victims of their socioeconomic and cultural circumstances. The proper perspective undoubtedly lies somewhere in between. Behavior surely matters, but so does the socioeconomic and physical environment.

As of this writing, the third version of the 2017 health reform bill that actually was passed by the House of Representatives (H.R. 1628) would leave it up to the states to decide whether they wish to impose community rating on insurance companies or allow them to set actuarially fair premiums. That provision was not included in the Senate draft bill H.R. 1628 Better Care Reconciliation Act of 2017.[5]

High-Risk Pools

When reminded that going back to pre-Obamacare, actuarially fair pricing might throw millions of relatively sick people off the insurance rolls, the defenders of actuarially fair premiums invariably mention that sicker Americans would be taken care of through so-called *high-risk pools*.

The problem with that riposte is twofold.

First, the history of high-risk pools in this country during the past several decades is strewn with pools that failed. The pools charged individuals premiums from 125 percent to 200 percent of the average premiums charged in the individual market and had very high deductibles and tight upper annual and lifetime limits. Furthermore, many of them were underfunded and limited enrollment to fit their underfunded budgets.

Second, politicians who allude to high-risk pools as a solution to the problems of chronically ill people (the jargon now is "people with pre-existing conditions") owe it to voters to spell out <u>precisely</u> the parameters they have in mind for their high-risk pool, to wit:

1. Precisely what will be the eligibility criteria to get into a high-risk pool?
2. What will be the premiums charged individuals accepted into the high-risk pool relative to the average premium charged in the individual market?
3. What are the specifics of the benefit package covered, which includes:
   a. Deductibles, coinsurance, and maximum annual risk exposure for enrollees
   b. Upper annual and lifetime limits on coverage
   c. Exclusions from coverage (e.g., maternity and newborn care, mental health care, and services for addicted people)
   d. Coverage of prescription drugs

Unless politicians proposing high-risk pools as a solution for people with serious pre-existing conditions are willing to provide voters with theses crucial details, they are effectively selling the voting public the proverbial pig in a poke. It should not be acceptable in a democracy.

Premium

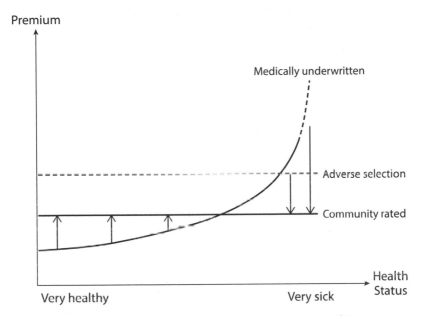

Figure 7.3 Medically Underwritten versus Community-Rated Premiums.

Community-Rated Premiums and the Death Spiral of Health Insurance

Figure 7.3 presents a hypothetical picture of actuarially fair and community rated premiums. It is only a rough sketch to make a point and is not based on real data. The curved line in the graph (designated "medically underwritten") depicts actuarially fair premiums, and the solid horizontal line (designated "community related") a community-rated premium, both lines for the same risk pool.

Because community rating clearly raises premiums of younger and healthier individuals above their true actuarial costs, these individuals have a strong incentive not to buy insurance, knowing that if they should fall seriously ill, they can then throw themselves upon the mercy of the *community-rated* premium. It is an open invitation to gaming the system, a maneuver actuaries call "adverse risk selection."

In the graph, the upward-shifted dashed line (designated "adverse selection") shows this effect. This higher community-rated premium will drive yet another cohort away from insurance coverage, which will further drive up the community-rated premium of the remaining, now much more expensive risk pool. Actuaries call this dynamic the "death spiral" of health insurance.

This death spiral is not just theory. It has been observed in real life in the states of New Jersey[6] and New York, both of which imposed community rating on insurers without also mandating that all individuals must acquire health insurance. Because this dire outcome was perfectly predictable, one must wonder what the legislators in these two states were thinking when they passed the relevant bills into law.[7]

If insurers must sell coverage to anyone willing to pay a community-rated premium, individuals must be strictly *mandated* to purchase such coverage. Such a mandate, in turn, requires that public subsidies be paid to or on behalf of those low-income individuals unable to afford the mandated coverage with their own financial resources.

This mandate will anger voters all along the ideological spectrum. Critics on the right see it as trampling on the freedom of Americans. Critics on the left sometimes interpret it as just a means to drive new customers into the arms of greedy insurance companies. In fact, the mandate is an actuarial necessity.

8

■

The Elephant in the Room and the Ethical Vision Baked into Health Reform Proposals

As has been noted elsewhere in the book, it is an unwritten rule that in this country we prefer to debate proposed health reforms mainly in terms of technical parameters—actuarially fair versus community-rated premiums, deductibles, coinsurance, maximum risk exposure, high-risk pools, and so on.

In fact, however, our arguments always have been, are now, and will continue forever to be over the elephant in the room no one likes to mention, namely, the fundamental question, *to what extent we should be our poor and sick brothers' and sisters' keepers in health care.*

The wrestling match over U.S. health reform during the past decade—and especially the drama that played out within the Republican Party in 2017—is over this fundamental question.

Most countries have confronted this question head on long ago and settled it. In the United States, we have never been able to reach a politically dominant consensus on the distributive social ethic that should guide our health system, because we dare not confront that question at all (see figure 8.1). By contrast, we in the United States have debated these ethical issues only in camouflaged form for over a century now, but have never

Figure 8.1 Americans Confronting the Ethical Dimension of U.S. Health Care.
Source: Alan Simpson/Alamy Stock Photo.

reached a politically acceptable consensus on the issue. The debate in 2017 on repealing and replacing Obamacare is merely a continuation of this camouflaged and confusing debate.

It is a question of social ethics, not of economics. Practically, the answers to this fundamental question express themselves in the particulars of the health reforms.

At one extreme, many Americans would like to see health care treated as a pure *social good*—like elementary and secondary education—to be available to all on roughly equal terms and financed by households on the basis of their ability to pay.

At the other extreme, many other Americans would like to see health care treated like any other basic, private consumption good—like food, clothing, and shelter—of which every American should be accorded a basic, bare-bones ration, but whose time-liness, quantity, and quality can be rationed by income class.

In between are millions of Americans who never give this issue any thought until they fall ill and face difficulties paying their medical bills; then they generally slouch toward the "social good" perspective on health care, unless they are very well insured or very rich.

Given the complexity of our health system, any health reform proposal contemplated by government is correspondingly complex, especially because those proposals involve ideological preferences. That complexity gave rise to a comment by President Trump that "Nobody knew that health care could be so complicated,"[1] although, after the stillbirth of the Clinton health reform plan in the 1990s and the breech birth of the Affordable Care Act of 2010 (Obamacare), he must have been the only one who did not know.

To health policy wonks, this author included, the details of health reform proposals are more titillating even than *Lady Chatterley's Lover.* Although the details of the various ill-fated health reform proposals fiercely debated within the Republican ranks in the summer of 2017 are moot at this time, these details convey the general thrust of the debate and, in particular, the ethical vision baked into them. They are therefore summarized and assessed in the next two chapters, starting with chapter 9 on the Affordable Care Act as a backdrop for comparisons. The discussion in chapter 10 on the House and Senate bills omits the plan submitted by Senators Bill Cassidy (R-LA) and Lindsey Graham (R-SC) in late September 2017 because it was basically more of the same. The discussion in chapter 10 also includes a brief look at how the nonpartisan Congressional Budget Office has "scored" the proposals as to fiscal impact and the number of uninsured.

9

∎

The Ethical Vision of the Affordable Care Act of 2010 (Obamacare)

The Affordable Care Act (Obamacare), a convenient summary of which can be found in the *Summary of the Affordable Care Act* published by the Kaiser Family Foundation in April 2013,[1] slouches in the direction of health care as a social good, but far from perfectly so.

Focus on the Poor

The Affordable Care Act definitely tries to direct the bulk of federal subsidies toward the lower levels of the income distribution, as can be inferred from the following provision:[2]

- Provide refundable and advanceable premium credits to eligible individuals and families with incomes between 100–400 percent FPL (federal poverty level) to purchase insurance through the Exchanges. The premium credits will be tied to the second lowest cost Silver plan in the area and will be set on a sliding scale such that the premium contributions are limited to the following percentages of income for specified income levels:[3]

Up to 133 percent FPL: 2 percent of income
133–150 percent FPL: 3–4 percent of income
150–200 percent FPL: 4–6.3 percent of income
200–250 percent FPL: 6.3–8.05 percent of income
250–300 percent FPL: 8.05–9.5 percent of income
300–400 percent FPL: 9.5 percent of income

- Increase the premium contributions for those receiving subsidies annually to reflect the excess of the premium growth over the rate of income growth for 2014–2018. Beginning in 2019, further adjust the premium contributions to reflect the excess of premium growth over CPI if aggregate premiums and cost sharing subsidies exceed .504 percent of GDP.
- Provide cost-sharing subsidies to eligible individuals and families. The cost-sharing credits reduce the cost-sharing amounts and annual cost-sharing limits and have the effect of increasing the actuarial value of the basic benefit plan to the following percentages of the full value of the plan for the specified income level:

100–150 percent FPL: 94 percent
150–200 percent FPL: 87 percent
200–250 percent FPL: 73 percent
250–400 percent FPL: 70 percent

Nevertheless, the Affordable Care Act still falls far short of the vision of health care as a pure *social good*. It still leaves millions of individuals in this country uninsured and saddles those who do have coverage with deductibles and coinsurance so high as to constitute effective financial barriers to needed care.

Besides, as already noted, the steep premium increases Obamacare has triggered have priced millions of American households with incomes above 400 percent of the federal poverty level out of health insurance. In fact, it is only for this *unsubsidized* group of Americans that Obamacare shows early symptoms of the *death spiral* in health insurance described earlier (chapter 7) in this book.

Neglect of the Middle Class

Countries that use community-rated premiums all have such mandates on individuals to be insured, which they strictly enforce, including garnishing people's wages.[4]

By contrast, the mandate to be insured baked into Obamacare was enforced in a way that made it much cheaper for healthy young individuals to pay the moderate penalties for disobeying the mandate than to purchase the mandated coverage. Consequently, premiums under Obamacare had shown early symptoms of a death spiral. Between 2016 and 2017 average premiums[5] rose by 22 percent, although the changes by region had shown a huge variance—increases of 116 percent in Arizona, 63 percent in Tennessee, and only 5 percent in New Jersey, and a negative (−3) percent decline in Massachusetts. As always, averages squeeze out important information.

These average *percentage* increases can also be confusing, because they do not tell us anything about the level of premiums. The actual premium for an individual in dollars was $422 per month in Arizona, even after a 116 percent increase in premiums. It was as much as $446 in North Carolina and $413 in Wyoming, where premiums increased by only 9 percent.[6] In other words, with its sharp premium increase, Arizona merely moved premiums in line with those charged in other states. It is all quite complicated and confusing.

The Assistant Secretary for Planning and Evaluation (ASPE) of the Department of Health and Human Services (DHHS) has written a detailed research paper on these data.[7]

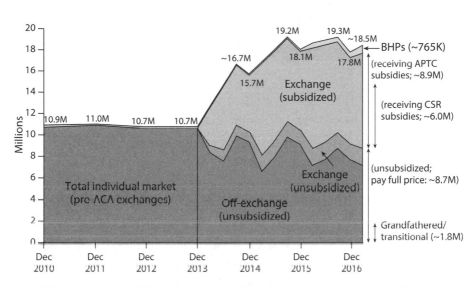

Figure 9.1 Total U.S. Individual Health Insurance Market, 2010–2016. *Source:* Total U.S. Individual Health Insurance Market 2010–2016, ACAsignups .net, Charles Gaba. Data from Mark Farrah Associates and the Centers for Medicare and Medicaid. Reprinted with permission.

These rapid increases in premiums under Obamacare have different impacts on two distinct groups of Americans.

1. They do not affect those Americans with adjusted gross incomes below 400 percent of the federal poverty level, who therefore receive federal subsidies.
2. They do, however, hit with full force Americans with adjusted incomes above 400 percent of the federal poverty level, or those who for one reason or another purchase health insurance in the off-Obamacare non-group market.

Figure 9.1, constructed by health policy analyst Charles Gaba, shows the number of individuals falling into these categories as of December 2016.

Subsidized Individuals on the Obamacare Exchanges

For the about 78 percent of Americans who have purchased health insurance on the Obamacare market exchanges (about 9.4 million people) and received federal subsidies toward the premiums for that coverage, these increases in total premiums under Obamacare are of no importance. Their contribution to these total premiums (called their "net premium" paid) is simply a fraction X of their adjusted gross income, where X rises with income and descends to 0 percent for individuals with an adjusted gross income of 400 percent or above of the federal poverty level (FPL).

Figure 9.2 shows how the federal poverty level (FPL) changes with family size and relates it to dollar figures for the year 2017.[8]

The fractions X of their income that households under 400 percent of the FPL are to contribute to their health insurance premiums rise with income, and each rises slightly over time. Since 2014, they have increased at an average annual compound growth rate of 0.66 percent.

Figure 9.3 shows how the fraction X varied with income in 2017.

Suppose, for example, that in a given county the second-lowest premium demanded by participating insurers for a Silver[9] plan for an individual aged forty is $400 a month, or $4,800 per year. Suppose next that the individual's adjusted gross income is $40,000 and that the individual's required contribution to the premium is 5.2 percent of that income, that is, $2,080 a year. Then the federal subsidy for that individual's health insurance coverage would be $4,800 − $2,080 = $2,720.

Government's total annual spending on premium subsidies under Obamacare may rise or fall when younger, healthier people choose to drop their Obamacare coverage. For households who

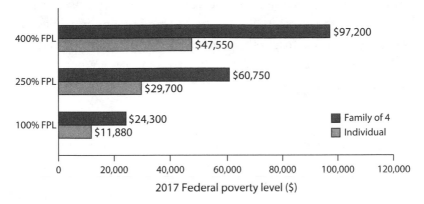

Figure 9.2 2017 Federal Poverty Levels in Dollars.
Source: ObamaCare Net, 2017 Federal Poverty Levels, https://obamacare.net/2017
-federal-poverty-level/.

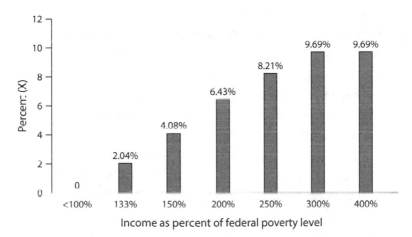

Figure 9.3 Percentage (X) of Modified Adjusted Gross Income (MAGI)
Households Pay toward Insurance Premium for Second-Cheapest Silver
Plan, 2017.
Source: The percentage cited in this graph is based on table 2: Premium Cap, by Income
in 2017 and 2018, in Kaiser Family Foundation. Explaining Health Care Reform:
Questions About Health Insurance Subsidies. Published Nov 08, 2017. https://www
.kff.org/health-reform/issue-brief/explaining-health-care-reform-questions-about
-health/.

remain insured, the government now pays higher subsidies per household. On the other hand, it no longer pays any subsidies for people who have dropped their insurance on the Obamacare exchanges, and it collects from them a penalty payment. How this nets out for taxpayers is an empirical question.

Unsubsidized Americans Purchasing Coverage in the Individual (Non-group) Market

Under Obamacare, the government does not pay any subsidies for individuals with an adjusted gross income of 400 percent or more of the federal poverty level. However, they all must pay the community-rated premiums established by the Obamacare exchanges for subsidized Americans. The high increases in the premiums charged by insurers for the second-cheapest Silver plan on the Obamacare markets therefore hit this unsubsidized higher-income group in full force.

This steep premium increase also hits in full force other Americans who for one reason or another prefer to purchase individual insurance off the Obamacare marketplace—an estimated 9 million Americans, of whom, curiously, 2.5 million would actually be entitled to federal subsidies[10] if they bought their coverage on the Obamacare exchanges.

Quite understandably, Republicans and other opponents of Obamacare have successfully made the plight of this group of close to ten million higher-income individuals the focus of their criticism. It is why they, and President Trump, argue that Obamacare is imploding, which actually does not apply to the market segment that receives federal subsidies. That market is not imploding.

However, Americans with incomes above 400 percent of the federal poverty level, or those who buy insurance in the off-Obamacare market, are hit fully by these sharp premium increases. For them the non-group market is imploding. It is a major shortcoming of Obamacare. So far, the defenders of Obamacare have swept the plight of these Americans too easily under the rug. In the political arena, it is risky to give short shrift to millions of voters who are being hosed by a legislation.

Fixing Obamacare

What fixes could be used to address this major shortcoming of Obamacare? One can think of several, all of them difficult to implement in the current political climate.

1. A technically easy but politically difficult fix would be to extend the public subsidies toward the purchase of health insurance further up the income ladder, say, to 500 percent or 600 percent of the federal poverty level. This would require added taxes and transfers.
2. Another technically easy but politically difficult fix would be to increase the penalty for remaining uninsured. This would not be politically popular and would undoubtedly lead to more litigation with uncertain[11] outcomes.
3. A third and so far untried approach would be to eschew a mandate to be insured altogether and instead to offer individuals a deal they might find hard to refuse. Under such a deal, individuals would be free to remain uninsured, but if they did so beyond a finite enrollment window, they could not avail themselves of the community-rated premiums charged on the Obamacare exchanges for, say, N years.

In my view, the third option is the best approach, as long as N is large enough. As I shall argue further on, in the conclusion of the book, a good case can be made for a lifetime ban on joining the community-rated market.

10

.

The Ethical Vision of the Health Reform Proposals of 2017

The Ethical Vision of H.R. 1628, the American Health Care Act of 2017 (AHCA)

H.R. 1628, known as the American Health Care Act (AHCA), passed by the U.S. House of Representatives in May 2017, clearly envisages a health system in which health care is substantially, if not wholly, rationed by price and the individual household's ability to pay for it.

Unlike the Affordable Care Act (ACA) of 2010 (Obamacare), which bases the magnitude of federal subsidies on *income*, under the AHCA these subsidies take on the form of refundable tax credits that vary only by age,[1] and not by income, as follows:

> Starting in 2020, replace ACA income-based tax credits with a flat tax credit adjusted for age. Credits are payable monthly. Annual credit amounts are as follows: $2,000 per individual up to age 29; $2,500 per individual for ages 30–39; $3,000 per individual for ages 40–49; $3,500 per individual for ages 50–59; $4,000 per individual for age 60 and older.

(For a convenient, crisp summary of the AHCA, see *Summary of the American Health Care Act*, published by the Kaiser Family Foundation.[2])

Furthermore, while individuals in the highest age bracket (before Medicare sets in) receive only twice the tax credit that is received by the youngest cohort, health insurers may charge that oldest age cohort up to five times the premiums charged the youngest cohort. Under Obamacare, that ratio has been only three to one.

Under the version of the AHCA that actually passed the House (H.R. 1628), states can opt to waive the requirements that insurers cover a specified "essential health benefits" (EHB) package at *community-rated* premiums. The states can let insurers specify the benefits package they wish to offer and to price it at *actuarially fair* (*medically underwritten*) premiums. States choosing that option would have to offer their citizens a *high-risk pool*, whose precise parameters, however, are not specified in the law.

Critics of the House bill have argued that benefits likely to be dropped from the EHB list by the states would be some mental health and substance abuse services and maternity care.[3] These benefits were frequently excluded from coverage in the non-group market prior to the launch of Obamacare. Some health policy analysts and politicians have explicitly raised objections to the requirement under Obamacare that single men or childless couples cover maternity care as part of the coverage they are required to buy. Conservative policy analyst Linda Gorman has styled Obamacare as "Obama's War on Men."[4] In an interview on Fox News, conservative policy analyst Avik Roy echoed that sentiment by calling Obamacare a "War on the Bros."[5] Congressman John Shimkus (R-IL) has openly expressed the same sentiment.[6]

Converting maternity and neonatal health care into a purely private good whose financing is the user's responsibility may be foolish from a longer-term perspective. In an op-ed column[7] in the *Washington Post*, Tsung-Mei Cheng and this author reminded readers of the large body of scientific research finding

Table 10.1 Congressional Budget Office Estimates on Two Versions of the AHCA Relative to Current Law (ACA of 2010, or Obamacare)

Impact on 2017–2026 on	Original AHCA[a] not voted on	Revised AHCA[b] passed by House, May 4, 2017
Federal Revenues	($882 billion)	($992 billion)
Federal Expenditures	($1,219 billion)	($1,111 billion)
Change in Deficit	($337 billion)	($119 billion)
Number of Uninsured by:		
2018	14 million more	14 million more
2020	21 million more	19 million more
2026	24 million more	23 million more

[a]Congressional Budget Office, American Health Care Act, March 13, 2017, Tables 1 and 5.
[b]Congressional Budget Office, H.R. 1628, American Health Care Act of 2017, May 24, 2017, Tables 1 and 4.

that the in utero experience of a fetus has a strong influence on that newborn's health into adulthood and even on that of the next generation.[8] If single men and childless couples are not to be required to help finance maternity and neonatal care through the health insurance premiums they pay, then a case can be made for financing that care publicly, as the United States now does for patients of all ages on renal dialysis. Medicare finances their care.

Finally, the AHCA passed by the House would eliminate most of the taxes on higher-income individuals called for by the Affordable Care Act to help finance the subsidies granted low-income households under that act. To help reduce the deficit in the face of these tax cuts, the AHCA calls for sizeable cuts in the federal contribution to the Medicaid program for the poor and for an overall reduction in the federal subsidies granted low-income Americans. Table 10.1 illustrates the overall impact of the original and the revised version of the AHCA on the fiscal situation and on the number of uninsured.

It does not require a PhD to recognize instantly that, relative to the Affordable Care Act of 2010, older, low-income individuals will fare much worse under the AHCA. More formal analyses support that intuition. A good side-by-side comparison of the Affordable Care Act and the AHCA, for example, is offered in a July 2017 *Los Angeles Times* article, "A Side-by-Side Comparison of Obamacare and the GOP's Replacement Plans,"[9] and in the Kaiser Family Foundation's March 2017 publication, *How Affordable Care Act Repeal and Replace Plans Might Shift Health Insurance Tax Credits.*[10] Table 10.1 exhibits some of the slight differences between the House bill that did not pass (the original AHCA bill not voted on) and the somewhat revised bill that did pass.

In its May 24, 2017, analysis of H.R. 1628 (the version of the AHCA actually passed by the House of Representatives on May 4, 2017), the nonpartisan Congressional Budget Office presented a table, table 10.2 here (which appeared as table 5 in the CBO report), showing the impact of the AHCA, relative to the ACA of 2010 ("Current Law" in table 5 of the CBO report), on individuals of a given age and income. For details on how this table was constructed, the reader is referred to the footnotes of the table.[11]

After some Talmudic contemplation of the CBO's table 5 (table 10.2 here), it should become clear that the AHCA is designed to shift the financial burden of health care away from healthier and wealthier individuals onto the shoulders of older and lower-income individuals.

It emerges from all of the side-by-side analyses of the AHCA of 2017 with the ACA of 2010 that what will happen to premiums and out-of-pocket costs for health care by households depends on the age of individuals and their income.

Statements based solely on *average* premiums—for example, "the AHCA will lower premiums"—are so simplistic as to be

Table 10.2 (CBO Report Table 5) Illustrative Examples of Subsidies in 2026 for Nongroup Health Insurance under Current Law and under H.R. 1628, the American Health Care Act, as Passed by the House of Representatives on May 4, 2017

Dollars

	Premium[a]	Premium Tax Credit[b]	Net Premium Paid
SINGLE INDIVIDUAL WITH ANNUAL INCOME OF $26,500 (175 PERCENT OF FPL)[c]			
Current Law			
21 years old	5,100	3,400	1,700
40 years old	6,500	4,800	1,700
64 years old	15,300	13,600	1,700
H.R. 1628 in an Illustrative State Not Requesting Waivers for Market Regulations			
21 years old	4,200	2,450	1,750
40 years old	6,550	3,650	2,900
64 years old	21,000	4,900	16,100
H.R. 1628 in an Illustrative State with Moderate Changes to Market Regulations			
21 years old	3,700	2,450	1,250
40 years old	5,750	3,650	2,100
64 years old	18,500	4,900	13,600
SINGLE INDIVIDUAL WITH ANNUAL INCOME OF $68,200 (450 PERCENT OF FPL)[c]			
Current Law			
21 years old	5,100	0	5,100
40 years old	6,500	0	6,500
64 years old	15,300	0	15,300
H.R. 1628 in an Illustrative State Not Requesting Waivers for Market Regulations			
21 years old	4,200	2,450	1,750
40 years old	6,550	3,650	2,900
64 years old	21,000	4,900	16,100
H.R. 1628 in an Illustrative State with Moderate Changes to Market Regulations			
21 years old	3,700	2,450	1,250
40 years old	5,750	3,650	2,100
64 years old	18,500	4,900	13,600

Source: H.R. 1628, American Health Care Act of 2017, https://www.cbo.gov/publication/52752.

nonsensical. There are major winners and losers under a repeal and replacement of the Affordable Care Act. Honorable persons would acknowledge it forthrightly.

Finally, the CBO also presented a neat visual explaining the changes in government revenue and spending under the AHCA relative to current law, that is, Obamacare (see figure 10.1). That display is self-explanatory.

The conclusion emerging from the CBO's table 5 (table 10.1 here) was reached in an earlier analysis of the first draft of the AHCA (which failed to pass the House but which is, in this regard, not much different from the version that did pass) published by the Kaiser Family Foundation.[12]

Figures 10.2 and 10.3, two of many presented in the Kaiser analysis, are indicative.

Conservative *Forbes* editor and columnist Avik Roy penned a column[13] entitled "GOP's Obamacare Replacement Will Make Coverage Unaffordable for Millions—Otherwise, It's Great."

Most curious in this regard are reports that President Trump, who in a Rose Garden ceremony praised H.R. 1628 as a "great plan" when it passed on May 4, 2017, later regarded that same law as "mean." As the *New York Times*[14] reported in a story on June 14, 2017:

> At a White House lunch with more than a dozen Republican senators, Mr. Trump alerted his guests that a bill passed by the House this spring—one he lauded last month in the Rose Garden as a "great plan" that was "very, very incredibly well-crafted"—was now "mean."

Apparently, Mr. Trump expected the Senate to craft a bill that is "generous, kind, and with heart."[15]

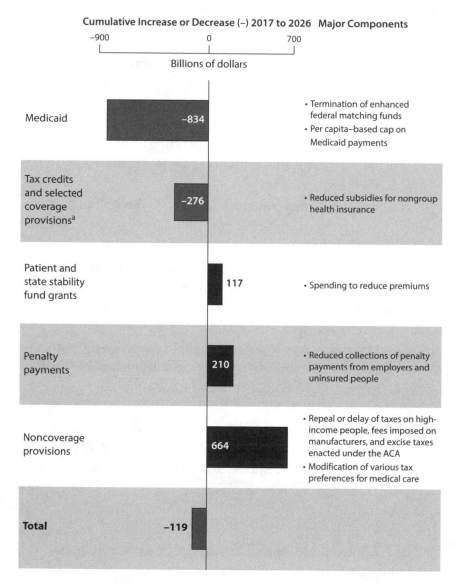

Cumulative Increase or Decrease (–) 2017 to 2026   Major Components

–900   0   700

Billions of dollars

Medicaid   –834
• Termination of enhanced
  federal matching funds
• Per capita–based cap on
  Medicaid payments

Tax credits
and selected
coverage   –276
provisions[a]
• Reduced subsidies for nongroup
  health insurance

Patient and
state stability   117
fund grants
• Spending to reduce premiums

Penalty   210
payments
• Reduced collections of penalty
  payments from employers and
  uninsured people

Noncoverage   664
provisions
• Repeal or delay of taxes on high-
  income people, fees imposed on
  manufacturers, and excise taxes
  enacted under the ACA
• Modification of various tax
  preferences for medical care

Total   –119

Figure 10.1 Net Effects of H.R. 1628 on the Budget Deficit. These estimates are for H.R. 1628, the American Health Care Act of 2017, as passed by the House of Representatives on May 4, 2017.
Source: H.R. 1628, American Health Care Act of 2017, https://www.cbo.gov/publication/52752.
ACA = Affordable Care Act.
a. Includes subsidies for coverage through marketplaces and related spending and revenues, small-employer tax credits, tax credits for nongroup insurance, Medicare, and other effects of coverage provisions on revenues and outlays.

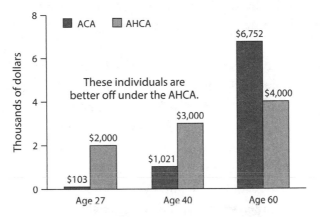

Figure 10.2 How the AHCA Might Shift Average Tax Credits by 2020, Individual's Income = $40,000.
Source: Cox, Clayton, and Levitt, http://kff.org/health-reform/issue-brief/how-afford able-care-act-repeal-and-replace-plans-might-shift-health-insurance-tax-credits/.

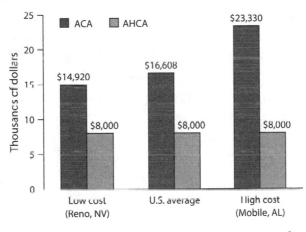

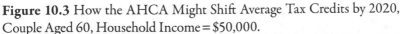

Figure 10.3 How the AHCA Might Shift Average Tax Credits by 2020, Couple Aged 60, Household Income = $50,000.
Source: Cox, Clayton, and Levitt, http://kff.org/health-reform/issue-brief/how-afford able-care-act-repeal-and-replace-plans-might-shift-health-insurance-tax-credits/.

The Ethical Vision of the Better Care Reconciliation Act of 2017 (BCRA)[16]

In a column published[17] in the *New York Times*, Drew Altman, president of the Kaiser Family Foundation, aptly described the Senate's draft bill, the H.R. 1628 Better Care Reconciliation Act of 2017 (BCRA) released by the Senate on June 22, 2017, as a "Jekyll-and-Hyde plan" that is "in some ways kinder than the House Republican plan [H.R. 1628], and in some ways meaner, to use President Donald Trump's yardstick."

On the "meaner" side are drastic cuts over the longer term in federal spending on the state-administered Medicaid program for poor adults under age sixty-five, the poor elderly, and blind and disabled Americans.

For Medicaid, the BCRA, like the House bill (the AHCA), would eliminate over time the very generous cost sharing the federal government under Obamacare offered states willing to enroll adults with incomes up to 133 percent of the federal poverty level into Medicaid. For the first few years, under Obamacare, the federal government assumed 100 percent of the cost of these new enrollees and 90 percent permanently thereafter. In effect, the federal government subsidized care for these new enrollees much more heavily than it did for the traditional enrollees—poor mothers and their children, the poor elderly, and the blind and disabled. One can see why this two-tier approach might rankle thoughtful people.

As of late 2017, thirty-one states had adopted this virtually free (for the states) Medicaid expansion.[18] Under the BCRA, the generous federal cost sharing for this expansion will gradually be pared back to the cost-sharing level for traditional Medicaid enrollees, which averaged 57 percent (more for poor states and less for rich states). The betting now is that many of the states that embraced the expansion of Medicaid would dial back on it under the BCRA if federal subsidies for the expansion to the states were pared back. The adults who would thus lose their Medicaid coverage would, however, be entitled to the income- and age-related federal subsidies under the BCRA. The question is whether they could afford the premium contribution required of them and the high deductibles and coinsurance baked into private insurance policies.

For all of Medicaid, the BCRA would convert the current arrangement of a federal match (an average of 57 percent of whatever states spent on Medicaid) to annual federal block grants or to per capita caps. These caps would increase from year to year by the medical care component of the urban Consumer Price Index (CPI) plus 1 percent until 2025, but thereafter only by the whole urban CPI, the so-called CPI-U.

This form of indexing is problematic, because health spending per capita has traditionally grown much faster than the CPI-U, as shown in figure 10.4, which presents the time path of per capita health spending[19] and the CPI-U[20] from 2000 to 2015, indexed to 1 for base year 2000.

There is every reason to believe that in the future the CPI-U also will grow more slowly than overall per capita health spending in the United States. Consequently, indexing the growth of the per capita Medicaid spending cap to the growth of the CPI-U will put enormous financial pressure on state governors and local health care providers.

It is one thing to try to peg the growth in per capita health spending for an entire national health system to some index, such as size of payroll on which insurance premiums are based (for example, Germany) or to the growth in GDP per capita. It is quite another matter to single out only one segment of the health sector for such a cap, especially when the growth of that cap is

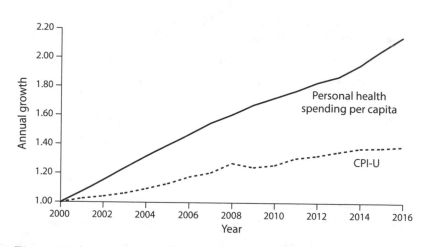

Figure 10.4 Annual Growth in Per Capita Health Spending and in the Consumer Price Index (CPIU), Year 2000 = 1.
Source: For health spending, Department of Human Services (DHHS), Centers for Medicare and Medicaid Services (CMS), "National Health Expenditure Accounts," available at https://www.cms.gov/research-statistics-data-and-systems/statistics-trends-and-reports/nationalhealthexpenddata/nationalhealthaccountshistorical.html. For the inflation rate, Inflation Data.com, Tim McMahon, "Historical Consumer Price Index (CPI-U)," October 13, 2017. https://inflationdata.com/Inflation/Consumer_Price_Index/HistoricalCPI.aspx?reloaded=true. Last viewed October 20, 2017.

pegged to an index that grows more slowly than does the growth of health spending in the rest of the health sector.

Health spending per capita is the product of health care utilization per capita and the prices of health care products and services. If health care prices rise faster than the entire CPI-U, then pegging the growth of per capita health spending under Medicaid will mean reductions in real health care utilization under Medicaid. It reminds one of Roberta Flack's "Killing Me Softly with His Song."[21] The "song" here is an arbitrary formula not easily defended on economic grounds.

There is nothing inherently wrong in converting the current open-ended federal match of Medicaid spending by the states into a risk-adjusted payment per Medicaid beneficiary. It all depends at what level that payment is set and how it will be allowed to grow over time.

A kinder and gentler approach would have been to set the *level* of the per capita payment per Medicaid beneficiary in a state to per capita spending by the private sector in that state, on a health status–adjusted basis. The *growth* in Medicaid spending per capita could then be set equal to the growth of private sector per capita spending, once again risk-adjusted. Here one should be mindful that the health status of Medicaid beneficiaries tends to be worse, on average, than that of, say, Americans with employment-based health insurance. As someone who has served on the board of a Medicaid managed care company, I know how challenging the Medicaid population can be.

There is, in fact, something bizarre about politicians who lament that Medicaid does not provide its beneficiaries with adequate access to health care, and that it provides lousy care to those who do find access, all the while voting for stingy budgets that force the states to pay doctors, hospitals, and other providers of health care very low fees—often so low as not even to cover the providers' costs. It is a bit like pushing grandmother down the stairs and then complaining that she is reckless.

On the *kinder* side, the Senate's BCRA[22] makes the tax credits toward the purchase of health insurance a function of both income and age, and not just of age, as the House bill (H.R. 1628) does. Thus, like Obamacare, it directs public subsidies more heavily than does the House bill toward lower-income Americans. Some people therefore have called it "Obamacare lite."[23]

Furthermore, the Senate bill would retain the Obamacare mandate on health insurers that they serve all applicants for insurance willing to pay the community-rated premium for a benchmark package of benefits. States could *not* opt out of this requirement. Under Obamacare, that community-rated premium was the *second-lowest* premium offered by insurers in the market area for a Silver policy, which would on average cover 70 percent of the actuarial cost of the mandated benefits. Under the BCRA, that benchmark premium would be the median for a benchmark policy designed, however, to cover only 58 percent, not 70 percent, of the actuarial cost of the benchmark package. By itself this provision would lower insurance premiums, but only because it covers less and drives up out-of-pocket spending. That lowering of the premium, however, would not be an achievement worth celebrating.

Given this lower coverage, one would expect the deductibles and coinsurance for insurance coverage under the BCRA to increase above the already high levels under Obamacare (averaging about $6,000 for an individual and $12,500 for a family[24]). Certainly, the CBO thinks so in its analysis of the BCRA. The additional Cost-Sharing Reduction (CSR)[25] payments under Obamacare, designed to help households below 250 percent of the FPL cope with out-of-pocket payments, would be continued under the BCRA only for the next two years. Thereafter, all households would be on their own in meeting their out-of-pocket medical expenses, which could be very burdensome for many low-income American households and might force them to forego health care they feel they need.

Table 10.3 is adapted from page 6 of the Senate's draft bill, showing the percentages of adjusted gross income (as a percentage of the federal poverty level) that the insured under the BCRA would have to contribute toward the insurance premium quoted by an insurer on the benchmark package, effective 2020.

In cells in the "age" columns in the table that show a range of values (for example, "2%–2.5%"), the first number represents the initial premium percentage—"percent of adjusted gross income the insured must contribute to their health insurance premium"—and the second number represents the final

Table 10.3 Percent of Adjusted Gross Income the Insured Must Contribute to their Health Insurance Premium under the BCRA and Obamacare

Adjusted Gross Household Income as Percent of the Federal Poverty Level	Under the Senate's Draft Better Care Reconciliation Act					Under Obamacare 2017	Under Obamacare estimated 2020
	Up to Age 29	Age 30–39	Age 40–49	Age 50–59	Over Age 59		
Up to 100%	2%	2%	2%	2%	2%	0%[a]	0%
100%–133%	2%–2.5%	2%–2.5%	2%–2.5%	2%–2.5%	2%–2.5%	2.04%	2.08%
133%–150%	2.5%–4%	2.5%–4%	2.5%–4%	2.5%–4%	2.5%–4%	3.06%–4.08%	3.12%–4.16%
150%–200%	4%–4.3%	4%–5.3%	4%–6.3%	4%–7.3%	4%–8.3%	4.08%–6.43%	4.16%–6.56%
200%–250%	4.3%	5.3%–5.9%	6.3%–8.05%	7.3%–9%	8.3%–10%	6.43%–8.21%	6.56%–8.37%
250%–300%	4.3%–6.4%	5.9%	8.05%–8.35%	9%–10.5%	10%–11.5%	8.21%–9.69%	8.37%–9.88%
300%–350%	4.3%–6.4%	5.9%–8.9%	8.35%–12.5%	10.5%–15.8%	11.5%–16.2%	9.69%	9.88%
350%–400%	**Full Premium**	**Full Premium**	**Full Premium**	**Full Premium**	**Full Premium**	9.69%	9.88%
Above 400%	**Full Premium**	**Full Premium**	**Full Premium**	**Full Premium**	**Full Premium**	**Full Premium**	**Full Premium**

Source: Congressional Budget Office.

[a] Under Obamacare, households up to 133% of the FPL were assigned to Medicaid, but only in states choosing the Medicaid Expansion (39 states as of this writing).

[premium] percentage for the particular income bracket in the table. "Initial" here refers to the income at the lower end of that income bracket, and "final" to the upper end of that bracket. These rates would become effective in 2020. The BCRA rates can be compared to the rates applicable under Obamacare in two ways. The first comparison is with actual Obamacare rates of 2017. The second comparison is with Obamacare rates projected to 2020 (the presumed effective date for the BCRA rates), assuming that the Obamacare rates will continue to increase slightly from year to year at their historical compound growth rate of 0.6627 percent per year.

The subsidy scheme under the Senate's BCRA clearly is similar to that used in Obamacare. However, it uses for the benchmark premium the *median* bid by insurers for a benchmark plan that covers only 58 percent of the actuarial cost of mandated benefits. Furthermore, federal subsidies toward the purchase of health insurance are granted only to individuals or households with adjusted gross incomes up to 350 percent of the federal poverty level ($41,580 for an individual or $85,050 for a household of four), not up to 400 percent, as in Obamacare.

Table 10.3 shows that for some younger, lower-income people, the BCRA would demand less of a contribution to their health insurance coverage than does Obamacare. For people above age forty or so, however, the BCRA would demand more of a contribution than does Obamacare. Compare, for example, the contribution rate people over age fifty-nine and with an income of 350 percent of the federal poverty level would have to make under the two schemes.

The BCRA has some additional tweaks of note.

First, as already noted, under Obamacare insurers are required to offer coverage to all comers willing to pay their premiums—which will continue to be *community rated*. States would not be allowed to opt out of this market arrangement, although they could use a waiver facility to change the definition of EHBs that must be covered by insurers.[26]

Second, the already weak mandate to be insured under Obamacare is eliminated altogether under the BCRA. Coupled with community-rated premiums, that is a prescription for the death spiral of insurance. Therefore, to give younger people an incentive to purchase insurance, the BCRA requires a six-month waiting period for anyone who has been uninsured for up to sixty-three days in the year, and a longer waiting period if the individual has been uninsured for more than sixty-three days. As the Congressional Budget Office's analysis[27] of the BCRA suggests, this provision still leaves considerable room for people to game the system through adverse risk selection against insurers.

Third, most of the taxes levied under Obamacare to help pay for the subsidies granted low-income Americans are eliminated under the BCRA. These have been taxes on investment income for households earning more than $250,000, a 0.9 percent surcharge on the Medicare payroll tax on high-income households, a tax on tanning salons, a tax on the health insurance industry, and a tax on the medical device industry.

Thus, like the House bill, the BCRA embodies the idea that significant portions of health care in America should be rationed by price and ability to pay, that is, by income class. That is a perfectly respectable position on the distributive ethic of health care. One only wishes that those who embrace the ethic would have the courage to state so openly for voters to understand.

In its analysis[28] of the BCRA (released on June 26, 2017), the Congressional Budget Office predicts that, relative to current law (that is, continuation of Obamacare), twenty-two million Americans will have lost health insurance coverage by 2026 under the BCRA, of which fifteen million are estimated to be fewer Medicaid enrollees (p. 16).

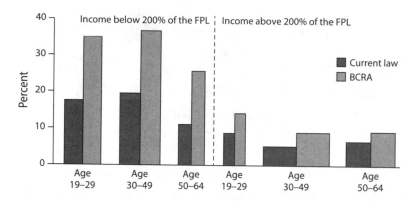

Figure 10.5 Share of Nonelderly Adults without Health Insurance Coverage under Current Law and the Better Care Reconciliation Act, by Age and Income Category, 2026. Estimates are based on CBO's March 2016 baseline, adjusted for subsequent legislation and reflect the average number of people under age 65 without insurance coverage over the course of the year in the noninstitutionalized civilian population of the fifty states and the District of Columbia. The width of each bar represents the relative share of the population in each age and income category. In CBO's projections, 200 percent of the FPL in 2026 would amount to $30,300 for a single person.
Source: H.R. 1628, Better Care Reconciliation Act of 2017, https://www.cbo.gov/publication/52849.
BRCA = Better Care Reconciliation Act of 2017 (a Senate amendment in the nature of a substitute to H.R. 1628).
FPL = federal poverty level.

Figure 10.5, taken directly from page 16 of the CBO analysis, provides further detail on this total. The dark gray bars represent current law (Obamacare). The lighter gray bars represent the BCRA. Evidently, relative to current law, the BCRA hits low-income Americans harder than it does higher-income Americans.

As the CBO is at pains to point out, these are merely plausible estimates most likely to occur. No pretense is made in the CBO analyses that these forecasts can be accurate a decade hence.

Table 10.4, also taken from the CBO analysis, shows the impact of the BCRA bill, relative to current law (Obamacare), for individuals in different circumstances. For details on the development of these scenarios the reader is referred to the footnote in the table.

The table shows, once again, how silly it is to describe the impact of a health reform bill on individuals by one simple metric, such as "Net premiums paid by Americans will decrease by 30 percent." Usually the impact is much more complex, with winners and losers. That fine point seems to elude almost all TV anchors and even many print pundits who commonly make bold but ignorant pronouncements on complex legislation.

Finally, the *fiscal implications* of the Senate and House bills, relative to current law (Obamacare), have been neatly explained by the CBO in figure 10.6.

The Senate bill would reduce cumulative *federal health spending* over 2017–2026 by about $1.1 trillion. That total is composed of $772 billion in cuts in federal spending off the projected growth in Medicaid spending under current law and $408 billion in reduced federal subsidies toward the purchase of private health insurance. On the other hand, the federal government would spend an extra $107 billion on grants to the states to help them reduce premiums for very-low-income Americans.

On the revenue side, the BCRA reduces cumulative revenues by a total of about $750 billion. Of that total, $541 billion would be from tax cuts, mainly for high-income Americans, and $210 billion would be from the elimination of penalties from individuals and business firms no longer required to pay these penalties under the BCRA.

Table 10.4 Illustrative Example of Subsidies for Nongroup Health Insurance in 2026 under Current Law and the Better Care Reconciliation Act of 2017 (Dollars)

	Bronze Plan				Silver Plan			
	Premium[a]	Premium Tax Credit[b]	Net Premium Paid	Actuarial Value of Plan (Percent)[c]	Premium[a]	Premium Tax Credit[b]	Net Premium Paid	Actuarial Value of Plan after Cost-Sharing Subsidies (Percent)[c]
SINGLE INDIVIDUAL WITH ANNUAL INCOME OF $11,400 (75 PERCENT OF FPL) AND NOT ELIGIBLE FOR MEDICAID[d,e]								
Current Law in a State Not Expanding Medicaid								
21 years old	4,300	0	4,300		5,100	0	5,100	
40 years old	5,500	0	5,500	60	6,500	0	6,500	70
64 years old	12,900	0	12,900		15,300	0	15,300	
BCRA in a State Not Expanding Medicaid								
21 years old	3,200	2,900	300		4,100	2,900	1,200	
40 years old	5,000	4,700	300	58	6,400	4,700	1,700	70
64 years old	16,000	15,700	300		20,500	15,700	4,800	
SINGLE INDIVIDUAL WITH ANNUAL INCOME OF $26,500 (175 PERCENT OF FPL)[d]								
Current Law								
21 years old	4,300	3,400	900		5,100	3,400	1,700	
40 years old	5,500	4,800	700	60	6,500	4,800	1,700	87
64 years old	12,900	12,900	0		15,300	13,600	1,700	

BCRA								
21 years old	3,200	1,900	1,300			4,100	1,900	2,200
40 years old	5,000	3,400	1,600	**58**		6,400	3,400	3,000
64 years old	16,000	14,000	2,000			20,500	14,000	6,500
								70

SINGLE INDIVIDUAL WITH ANNUAL INCOME OF $56,800 (375 PERCENT OF FPL)[d]

Current Law								
21 years old	4,300	0	4,300			5,100	0	5,100
40 years old	5,500	0	5,500	**60**		6,500	0	6,500
64 years old	12,900	8,500	4,400			15,300	8,500	6,800
								70

BCRA								
21 years old	3,200	0	3,200			4,100	0	4,100
40 years old	5,000	0	5,000	**58**		6,400	0	6,400
64 years old	16,000	0	16,000			20,500	0	20,500
								70

SINGLE INDIVIDUAL WITH ANNUAL INCOME OF $68,200 (450 PERCENT OF FPL)[d]

Current Law								
21 years old	4,300	0	4,300			5,100	0	5,100
40 years old	5,500	0	5,500	**60**		6,500	0	6,500
64 years old	12,900	0	12,900			15,300	0	15,300
								70

BCRA								
21 years old	3,200	0	3,200			4,100	0	4,100
40 years old	5,000	0	5,000	**58**		6,400	0	6,400
64 years old	16,000	0	16,000			20,500	0	20,500
								70

Source: H.R. 1628, Better Care Reconciliation Act of 2017, https://www.cbo.gov/publication/52849.

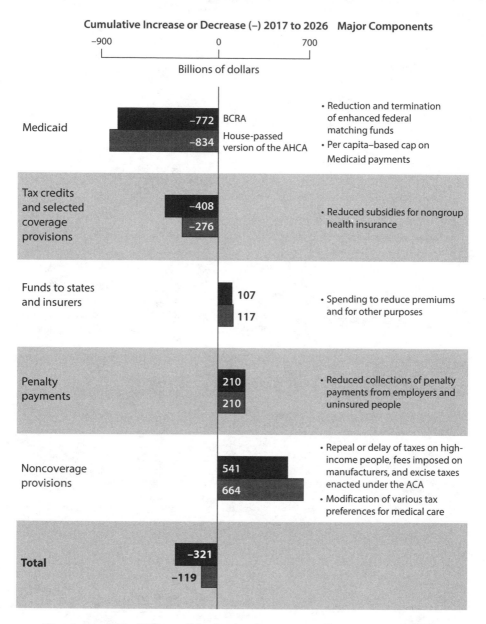

Figure 10.6 Net Effects of the Better Care Reconciliation Act and of the House-Passed Version of the American Health Care Act on the Budget Deficit.

Source: H.R. 1628, Better Care Reconciliation Act of 2017, https://www.cbo.gov /publication/52849.

These numbers imply a cumulative reduction in the deficit of about $320 billion over the decade.

All told, then, the Senate's BCRA, like the House bill (AHCA), does redistribute income from lower-income and sicker Americans toward younger, healthier, and wealthier Americans.

Although the Senate draft bill does grant American households income-based subsidies toward the purchase of health insurance—not only age-based subsidies, as in the House bill—the total amount of subsidies granted is projected to be lower than what would have been available under Obamacare. Eventually the bill would expose lower-income Americans to far higher deductibles and coinsurance than they already would have faced under Obamacare, leading to more self-rationing of health care over price and their ability to pay.

Policy analysts and media pundits positioned on the left of the ideological spectrum naturally look askance at the Senate's bill. It certainly does not conform to their professed ethical precepts for health care.

Among conservatives, the reception has been mixed, even among Senate Republicans.

Conservative policy analyst Avik Roy, who had earlier criticized[29] the House bill, opined[30] in the *Washington Post* that the Senate bill "will, if passed, represent the greatest policy achievement by a Republican Congress in generations." The same passionate support for the bill comes across in a June 26, 2017 interview with Dylan Scott of *Vox*.[31]

On the other hand, conservative *New York Times* columnist Ross Douthat argues, in a June 24, 2017 column entitled "From Worse to Bad on Health Care,"[32] that "stinginess is still the essential problem for the Senate alternative" and that "the Senate's health care bill deserves to fail." Conservative *New York Times* columnist David Brooks echoes this view in his June 27, 2017 column "The G.O.P. Rejects Conservatism."[33]

The Cruz Amendment

Senator Ted Cruz (R-TX) has introduced an amendment to the BCRA that would allow health insurers that do offer policies in compliance with the strictures of Obamacare also to offer policies that do not comply with those strictures.

These alternative, noncompliant policies could have skimpier benefit packages and could be priced on an actuarially fair basis, not a community-rated basis. In other words, they could revert to the market conditions in the non-group market (servicing about twenty million Americans) that existed before the onset of Obamacare. Presumably these policies would be purchased primarily by healthy people who would be reasonably well served with catastrophic policies that cover only expenses above a high deductible threshold. Therefore, healthier individuals with these alternative, noncompliant policies should experience substantial declines in their health insurance premiums relative to the current Obamacare exchanges. The question, of course, is what happens when previously healthy people with skimpy, low-premium policies fall seriously ill and then need expensive treatments (for example, very expensive biological drugs) that are not covered by the skimpy policies. Will they then be rationed out of these treatments, or will hospitals be obliged to deliver them as uncompensated charity care?

The Obamacare insurance exchanges with a stipulated, more comprehensive benefit package priced at community rate would continue to exist under the Cruz amendment. Because they would be used primarily by relatively sicker individuals, these exchanges would effectively function as automatic high-risk pools.

Individuals with incomes up to 350 percent (under the BCRA) or 400 percent (under Obamacare) of the federal poverty level in these high-risk pools are required to pay only a fraction X of their income toward the premium for these policies.

That arrangement would continue under the Cruz amendment. Therefore, these individuals would continue to be insulated from the death spiral that might be unleashed by adverse risk selection on the part of the insured. Taxpayers would pick up the difference between the high premiums and the contributions by subsidized individuals.

Relatively sick individuals in the high-risk pools with incomes above 350 percent or 400 percent of the federal poverty level, however, would bear the full brunt of the rapid increases that adverse risk selection would trigger under community-rated premiums.

Although at the time of this writing the details of the Cruz amendment have not been fully worked out, the idea seems to have one flaw. As noted, the arrangement invites continued adverse risk selection on the part of individuals and potential free-loading. For that reason, I would impose a more stringent set of requirements on individuals, as explained in the conclusion of the book.

The (Probably Temporary) Demise of Health Reform in the Senate

In late July 2017, leaders of the Senate introduced several versions of health reform only to see them voted down. Finally, in the early morning hours[34] of July 28, the Senate, by one vote, rejected a final-straw bill, known as the "skinny repeal,"[35] which would have allowed the Senate to combine with the House in conference to hash out a new health reform bill acceptable to both chambers. With that vote, health reform in the Congress was temporarily laid to rest, at least until after Congress's August recess.

As of late 2017, it remained to be seen how soon the Republican Congress can assemble enough votes to pass a health reform bill that can pass muster with the American public. Much would hinge on the outcome of the 2018 midterm election, as health care has emerged as a major campaign issue as it has been in many recent elections in the United States. If the Republicans retained control of the Congress, it would be reasonable to assume that efforts to repeal and replace the Affordable Care Act of 2010 would continue. On the other hand, loss of control of one or both chambers of the Congress would change the debate on health care in the United States. Republican efforts to repeal and replace the Affordable Care Act would be put on hold, but many expect them to continue their efforts to disrupt key elements of the Affordable Care Act. One sure thing that everyone can expect is that there will be major competing health care reform initiatives emerging from both the Republican and Democratic parties and candidates ahead of the 2020 presidential election.

Conclusion
A Novel (My Own) Reform
Proposal: Give Rugged
Individualists Their Freedom

In an article penned in 2009, before the Affordable Care Act of 2010 had been fully composed, Princeton sociologist Paul Starr[1] had warned the designers of that act to forego the controversial mandate on individuals to be insured. He proposed instead that individuals who failed to purchase health insurance during an initial time window should be barred for five years from the community-rated Obamacare exchanges.

Although I agree with that approach, a penalty period of only five years strikes me as much too short. Therefore, in a *New York Times* column entitled "Social Solidarity vs. Rugged Individualism,"[2] I had proposed that by age twenty-six all Americans must choose either to

a) join an insurance arrangement that forces on them *community-rated* premiums or, alternatively,
b) take a chance on being uninsured or relying on a health insurance market with premiums based on the individual's health status. If they chose the *rugged individualist* route,

Figure C.1 Beware the Uninsured Rugged American Individualist.
Source: George Rinhart/Corbis Historical/Getty Images.

however, they could never later on join the *social solidarity pool*.[3] They would be on their own throughout their life. That scheme would accommodate Libertarians who do not wish to be told by the government what to do about their health insurance.

By choosing to join the *social solidarity* pool, young Americans would know that the premiums they pay when young and healthy exceeded their actuarially expected cost of health care, but that they then will be paying premiums far below actuarial costs when they are older and sicker. It would be the health insurance analogue of buying a call option on a stock.

Rugged individualists who had chosen to go uninsured, or to rely on *medically underwritten* premiums, would know that they could lose all of their assets should they fall seriously ill. If they did fall ill or had a serious injury (see figure C.1) and then could not pay for their care, Medicaid would cover them, because rugged individualists live in a society that does not like to see people dying in the street.

However, should a rugged individualist receive health care under Medicaid, the government would set up an account for him or her to which would be charged all of their medical expenditures, priced at Medicare rates. The government would then have a claim on whatever subsequent assets the rugged individualist might accumulate, up to the debit balance in that individual's health care account. Libertarians should like this arrangement. To the objection that age twenty-six is too young an age to have to make such a monumental lifetime decision, I would respond that we ask young Americans entering military service to make a far more serious choice, one that may risk their limb and life.

EPILOGUE

Tsung-Mei Cheng

Health Reform for a Kinder America

The issue of universal coverage is not a matter of economics.
Little more than 1 percent of GDP assigned to health could
cover all. It is a matter of soul.
  —*Uwe E. Reinhardt*

Knowing is not enough; we must apply. Willing is not
enough; we must do.
  —*Johann Wolfgang von Goethe*

As a small boy in Germany, escaping a chase by his older brother,
Uwe Reinhardt ran full force into a large bowl his mother was
carrying and broke it. The sharp shards sliced into a blood vessel
in Uwe's neck and caused blood to spout out like an open spigot.
With his mother's hand firmly pressed against the pulsating
blood vessel, mother and child ran to the village doctor, where-
upon the doctor performed emergency treatment, without anes-
thesia: he closed the open cut with bare metal staples, which
stopped the hemorrhaging.

A native of Germany, Uwe lived his early years in wartime and postwar Germany, where he was exposed to both the excitement of playing with live ammunition found while roaming the gentle hills where the Reinhardt family lived and to the horrors of seeing Allied planes shot down and village children mowed down by indiscriminate Allied bombing and strafing in the German countryside. He learned at a young age that much of what happens to one in life is beyond one's control.

There are numerous examples of close encounters with high danger for the five young Reinhardt children, as they seemed to take turns coming down with serious life-threatening childhood infectious diseases. Each time, Uwe and his brothers and sisters were saved. How? Because his family had access to needed medical care, made possible and available to *all* Germans, rich or poor, by the social insurance system German chancellor Otto von Bismarck established in 1883. Germans may not always have had enough food in those years, but all had the health care they needed.

Uwe left Germany, alone, when he became of draft age because, as he said, "I refuse to salute German generals!" Arriving in Montreal, Canada, with ninety dollars in his pocket and ten years of German education, he worked as a clerk at a shipping company. To augment his miserly pay, he worked a second job as a parking lot attendant at night. For three years, Uwe lived the life of a working stiff in the large metropolis, with all its trials and tribulations. Once he saved enough money to attend the cheapest university in Canada at the time, he left for Saskatchewan—"I went to the Bank of Montreal and looked at the pamphlets to find the cheapest college, which was [the University of] Saskatchewan, and that's where I went"[1]—graduating four years later as winner of the Canadian Governor General's Gold Medal (Canada is a Commonwealth nation of the British Empire) with a degree in commerce and economics. His career goal then was to work for a corporation so that he would never be poor again, so he thought. One of his professors, however, had other plans for him, which put Uwe on a life course unimagined in his or his family's wildest dreams. He followed his professor's advice and went to Yale, on a scholarship, for graduate studies in economics.

The incomparably rich intellectual milieu of Yale gave Uwe the opportunity to study under titans of the field, including James Tobin, the Nobel laureate in economics and one-time economic adviser to President John F. Kennedy, and laid the foundation for Uwe's becoming, later on, a great health economist, teacher, and public intellectual.

As a public intellectual, Uwe engaged constantly with the public and the policy community. For many years Uwe wrote a regular column for the *New York Times Economix* blog, where he shared his thoughts and knowledge with readers on myriad topics going far beyond health care.

Uwe was also a committed teacher at heart, having taught at Princeton for nearly fifty years and being recognized as one of the most beloved professors in Princeton's history[2]—so writing this book for the American public and policy makers makes perfect sense. He often spoke about achieving Aristotelian human flourishing through education. It was Uwe's hope that the book will teach Americans about their highly complex health care system, so complex that it "is almost beyond human comprehension."

In *Priced Out*, Uwe takes you on what he called "a visual stroll through America's health care wonderland," which was the original title of the manuscript for the book. Uwe walks you through the "curious" and often "bizarre" American health care system, and explains why health care in America is so very expensive— and for millions of Americans downright unaffordable—and how the high cost of American health care has priced millions of

Americans out of needed health care. As he would often say, "Our health system is in danger of pricing kindness out of our souls."[3] He also shows that despite being the highest spenders on health care in the world, Americans actually do not receive more health care than citizens of wealthy nations in Europe or Asia. Americans simply pay much higher prices for all health care goods and services than people in any other country.

Furthermore, and importantly, Uwe walks you through the major health reform initiatives in America in recent years, including the Affordable Care Act (Obamacare) and the health reforms bills proposed in 2017 by our legislative representatives in both chambers of Congress.

Uwe has discussed those legislative initiatives at some length in the book, with a view to preparing readers to understand future legislative initiatives and their impact on individuals and families. As of the writing of this epilogue, ahead of the 2020 U.S. elections, Congress, think tanks, and industry groups are already busily preparing reform proposals to present to the American public. For example, the Senate health committee chair, Senator Lamar Alexander (R-TN), is already soliciting reform proposals from different sources and laying plans to address the issue of high health care costs in the United States in early 2019.

After reading *Priced Out*, readers may either be inspired, or angered, or disgusted by what they have learned from the book about health care in America, or feel some measure of all of the above. For those thinking of or perhaps willing and wanting to participate in the national dialogue and efforts to reform health care but wondering how and what they might do as citizens to help make a difference, the remarkable 2018 midterm election outcomes provide an excellent example, or road map.

For many years, Uwe warned that America is "sailing into the perfect storm" because of the high cost of health care, which leaves tens of millions of Americans uninsured. He also asked,

"Who will come to the rescue?" I believe the American public has an important role to play here. A key lesson from the 2018 midterm election is that when citizens become engaged, changes happen. And when *informed* citizens become engaged, big changes can happen for the good of society as a whole.

As readers, you can also engage in intelligent discussions on health policy at home with family, at school with teachers and classmates, at the workplace with colleagues and friends, at social gatherings, at town hall meetings, and at election campaign gatherings. You can also communicate directly with your own legislative representatives at the local, state, and even federal levels, or in the public sphere in the form of articles and opinions in newspapers and the media.

As a health policy analyst myself, I have personally found it useful to hear what top experts have to say on issues to inform my own thinking on those issues. Uwe certainly has been my most important teacher by far. To the extent that readers might also find it helpful to know what top health policy experts have to say about some of the most important but often puzzling issues regarding health care and health policy in America, I take the liberty here to share below, not in any particular order, what Uwe said and thought about some of them, based on interviews, congressional testimony, and some of Uwe's own writings. For decades, Uwe was thought of as "the premier health economist in the country... quoted widely on health care. Reinhardt is an expert on corporate finance and economic theory as well as health economics, a field in which he has become one of the definitive media sources. He is quoted frequently on everything from high drug prices to wasteful health spending."[4] As there have also been some new data out on U.S. health care spending and trends since *Priced Out* was written, I present them in the appropriate sections below. Here Goethe's famous words ring a bell: "Knowing is

not enough; we must apply. Willing is not enough; we must do."
Knowing is the first, preparatory step to applying and doing.

On universal health coverage. First, there can be no argument
that Uwe passionately believed in *universal health coverage* (UHC),
that is, health insurance that provides affordable and timely
access to needed health care for *all* regardless of the individual's
ability to pay, as a moral imperative. Deeply troubling to Uwe
since coming to America and studying health care was seeing so
many hard-working and less fortunate Americans not getting
their fair share in so rich a nation with so luxuriously endowed
a health care system as the American system. Time and again,
Uwe pronounced:

> What have we Americans become as a people to allow so
> much callousness and outright cruelty in a health system that
> is abundantly endowed with resources—in many instances
> excessively well endowed—and, as most Americans must
> know, also is home to much human kindness and excellence?

He said often, plain and simple:

> I grew up in a toolshed, and I know how good it was [that
> even] when we were paupers, my family . . . had health
> insurance like everyone else in Germany. I've never forgot-
> ten that. And I would like American people to have what
> I had and my mother had as a kid. So that is why I care.

His lifelong advocacy for UHC earned him broad respect.
Perhaps it was Uwe's compassion and respect for fellow Ameri-
cans that prompted Drew Altman, president and CEO of the
Henry J. Kaiser Family Foundation, to write this about Uwe:[5]

Uwe Reinhardt was a giant in our field, a moral compass for American health care. . . . Uwe always sought the truth. He always reminded us that behind all the data and graphs he loved so much were people. In doing that, he set the standards for all of us in health care.

On pressing issues concerning health care the Trump presidency faces. Uwe said this in a September 2016 interview by Princeton University:[6]

There still are millions of Americans who do not have health insurance of any kind, paying out of pocket for health care they need (if they have the money) or relying on charity care where available. Many Americans, although not all, view that as a social problem public policy should address. Even Americans who have procured health insurance through the ACA often find themselves saddled with high deductibles and coinsurance that makes access to needed health care difficult. It is a uniquely American problem.

The problem is exacerbated because we have the most expensive health system in the world, with prices twice as high or higher for identical health care goods (especially drugs) and services.

The U.S. health system has been carefully structured, often through enabling legislation triggered by special interest groups, to allow the supply side of the health care sector to extract enormous sums of money from the rest of society. Nowhere is this clearer than with specialty drugs, whose prices per year of treatment now routinely exceed $100,000. Yet on Capitol Hill, this system has always had its staunch defenders, for obvious reasons.

On health care cost growth. Uwe had repeatedly pointed out to Americans over the years what he called the "secret 2½ percent rule." As he wrote in 2009:[7]

> Over the past four decades, the growth of health spending has exceeded the growth of GDP *on average* by over two to two-and-a-half percentage points. The health sector has always marched on like that, like a stubborn and unstoppable beast.

Data on health spending and its projected growth reported in 2018 support Uwe's long-held observation. According to a February 2018 report by the Centers for Medicare and Medicaid Services (CMS) of the Department of Health and Human Services,[8] under the current law (the Affordable Care Act, or Obamacare), projected growth in total national health spending for 2018 is 5.3 percent of the United States' GDP, which reflects a sharp rise from 2016 and 2017, when it grew by 4.8 and 3.9 percent, respectively. GDP growth, on the other hand, again lagged behind growth in health spending by about 2 percent. To wit, GDP grew 1.5 percent in 2016 and 2.3 percent in 2017; and, according to updated projections (as of December 29, 2018) by the Congressional Budget Office, the U.S. GDP will grow 3.1 percent in 2018.[9] The CMS expects the 5.5 percent annual growth for health care spending to continue through 2026, when total U.S. health spending is estimated to reach 19.7 percent of the U.S. GDP. Once again Uwe's two-and-a-half percent rule is evident.

For many years, Uwe was concerned about the longer-term impact of the high cost of the American health system—the largest sector of the U.S. economy—on the country. He worried that if nothing is done to make the system more efficient—better cost control, better coverage, better access, better quality of care—health care, like Pac-Man, an analogy he liked to use, will simply continue to chew up more and more of the American economy, at great expense to America's other, competing national needs, such as education, infrastructure, the environment, national defense, R&D, and so on.

On common misconceptions about the Affordable Care Act (ACA). President Trump pledged to "repeal and replace" the ACA during his presidential campaign in 2016, and Congress tried to do that in 2017 but failed. Despite a court ruling by a judge in Texas in December 2018 that the ACA is "unconstitutional," the ACA is here to stay for the foreseeable future, as it has grown rather popular among Americans. It is important, however, to note some common misconceptions about the ACA, as Uwe pointed out in a Princeton University interview in November 2016:[10]

> Everyone seems to believe that *Obamacare* is all pervasive throughout the United States health system. It is not. It covers a small appendix of the United States system—the market for individually purchased health insurance and that for small business firms—hardly touching employment-based health insurance (which covers about two-thirds of the United States population and one-third of total health spending), Medicare, Tricare, the Veterans Health Administration system, etc. *Obamacare* is just a smallish, complicated and somewhat ugly patch onto a hugely complicated and hugely ugly health care financing system. . . .
>
> Another misperception is that *Obamacare* has been inflationary. In fact, it added less than 4 percent to what we would have spent on health care even in the absence of the ACA. The premium hikes we see in *Obamacare* now

(the premiums for 2017 relative to those for 2016) reflect three things: many (perhaps most) private insurers under-priced their policies, either by error or to gain market share, in the early years, a chicken that now comes home to roost; government assistance to compensate for higher than anticipated risk (called risk corridors) [was] yanked by Congress; and within age bands, fewer healthy people enrolled than had been hoped for, leaving the insurance risk pools on the market place exchanges with sicker people who cost more to treat.

Here it must be remembered that health spending is highly skewed. The top most costly 1 percent of Americans account for 21 percent of total national health spending, the top 5 percent for 51 percent, while the least costly 50 percent [account] for only 3 percent.

On prospects for universal health coverage in the United States. Years ago Uwe warned that America was "at a cross-roads" with regard to covering every American with health insurance because of the unstoppably high health spending. Writing in 2009, Uwe warned:

> Sometime during the coming decade, Americans will have to decide between two choices: first, whether they are willing to vote for a sizable tax-and-transfer program in health care (about $125 billion a year) to help finance health care for families in the bottom half of the income distribution, or, second, formally embrace rationing health care by income class, perhaps through *reference pricing* all around.

Uwe saw this policy divide more than a decade ago, and that was precisely what happened in the decade that followed: the Affordable Care Act, which was passed in 2010 and implemented in 2014, embraced the first choice; the Republican health reform proposals of 2017, the second.

The CMS estimates (2018) that by 2026 there will be more Americans without health insurance, rising from 8.9 percent of the U.S. population in 2016 to 10.7 percent of the population, a sizable increase. This will be largely due to a change in the Affordable Care Act that eliminated the individual mandate effective January 2019. President Obama's Affordable Care Act brought the total number of uninsured in the United States from 44 million in 2013, or approximately 17 percent of the U.S. population, to just below 27 million (or 8.9 percent) in 2016. However, the number of people without health insurance increased by nearly 700,000 in 2017, rising to 10.2 percent of the U.S. population.[11] These are worrisome trends.

On health care rationing, reference pricing, and America's health workforce. The United States is a country where one's socioeconomic status pretty much defines one's health care experience. Unlike citizens in most other rich nations, where everyone receives the same care, in the United States rationing of health care is a fact of life. Uwe pointed out time and again that despite the rhetoric so often heard in America that everyone is "equal," facts simply do not support that claim. The bottom line is that while the rich in America—Uwe called them "the aristocracy"—have excellent health care, for the poor and near-poor the opposite of that often is the case. Today, even for many, many Americans with health insurance, financial barriers often stand between them and the health care they need. On rationing of care Uwe said this in a lengthy C-SPAN interview in 2009, and it remains true today:[12]

Yes, there is no question we are rationing health care now. Usually we do it by price and ability to pay[;] for example, for an uninsured person, health spending is about half of what it is for a similar insured person. There is got to be rationing in there. So we already do it. . . . We are cruising into a world with a shortage particularly of primary care physicians, but also of certain specialties. And the age of the physician population is high—in the 50's. In other words, there haven't been enough young people [going into medicine]. I do not know why this country has not built more medical schools. To me, that's nuts, when a country is growing. And, so how will we close the gap? Well, we simply imported physicians trained in other countries, robbing them of their physicians. So I think our whole health workforce policy has been less than smart. I don't want to say stupid 'cause it's a little brash, but less than smart. And, it's also been less than fair to other countries, 'cause we're robbing them of their nurses, we are robbing them of their doctors. Maybe now we're expanding medical school capacity a little bit, but it's rather late for the game. So, yes, there will be rationing. And, Massachusetts is one of the over-doctored states, but there you cannot get a primary care physician even if you're rich. So it's already upon us.

But I think rationing will also take yet other means in the coming years, for example, there is in Germany and other countries a system called reference pricing for drugs. So what they do is they group all the drugs that attack a certain illness, say, blood pressure. They group them all into one therapeutic group. The insurance company says we'll pay a low-cost drug fully—maybe not the cheapest— but a low cost drug fully. If you want a more expensive brand name drug you pay the whole difference out of your own pocket. This is called reference pricing. You could do this to hospitals. The insurance company can say every time a patient goes there, it's very expensive; this other hospital is a lot cheaper, [so] we'll cover you fully if you go to that other hospital. If you go to the expensive one, you pay the whole difference out of pocket. You can do this with doctors. And you can just see how gradually, over time, you could just use this reference price system to say, for the poor, for you we have these low cost doctors, low cost hospitals, low cost drugs; and if you want Disneyland, you pay for it out of pocket. That, too, is a form of rationing that goes particularly along very well suited to our aristocracy. I am really quite serious that America has evolved into something of an aristocracy with a corporate elite that's completely divorced from the rest of American life and experience. They never take a subway, they never even take a cab. They got their own limos. They never take an airplane that isn't theirs, and they have lost touch with the American people.

On future prospects on health reform (insurance and financing reform) in the United States. Uwe believed that the United States will continue to "muddle through" as it always has, unless Americans somehow manage to reach a consensus on the distributive social ethics on health care. In the November 2016 interview by Princeton University, Uwe said this about health reform going forward:[13]

A major problem has been that the Republican opponents of the ACA have been very good at criticizing this or that feature of the ACA and thus defining it in the public's mind, but they have not been able to agree on a concrete replacement proposal of their own, aside from enunciating sets of principles that cannot be costed out by the Congressional Budget Office nor would allow one to describe to families how they would fare under particular circumstances. Republicans in this regard have been like drunken lovers at a bar: big talk, little action. . . . The best Americans can hope for is muddling through inelegantly, as we always have. One would hate to be lower-income in that system. Our health care financing system will always remain a horrendous mess and a fountain for such dismay among the providers of health care as well as among patients. We might as well get used to it: Americans will never have a health insurance system that does not confuse and anger people deeply, just as you cannot grow wheat at the North Pole. It's a state of nature.

On a single-payer Medicare-for-all system for America. Many have wondered about what Uwe might say about a single-payer system for the United States. The year 2018 saw a growing number of Americans warming to the idea of a single-payer Medicare-for-all health system. Here readers may be surprised by Uwe's take on a single-payer Medicare-for-all health system for the United States. In 1989, Uwe recommended the single-payer system to Taiwan when Taiwan's government was seeking to implement universal health insurance. Taiwan's government accepted Uwe's recommendation—at the time he dubbed it the "Single-Pipe System," as no one in Taiwan's government knew what a single-payer system was, but everyone understood what a plumber's "single pipe" is—and went on to build a single-payer system which has been highly successful and popular. However, Uwe was not optimistic about the prospect of a single-payer system in the United States.

Uwe told Harris Meyer of *Managed Care* in a 2013 interview that if Senator Bernie Sanders were to present his Medicare-for-all plan to Congress, it would be "dead on arrival" because "politically, you cannot legislate what rationally makes perfect sense."[14]

Washington Post columnist Ezra Klein, in a 2013 article, "Is the U.S. Too Corrupt for Single-Payer Health Care?," most clearly explained Uwe's views on single-payer and why he had not advocated the single-payer model for the United States:[15]

> Princeton's Uwe Reinhardt, a single-payer supporter, made an interesting variant of this argument: The reason the United States shouldn't have a single-payer system, he said, is that it's too captured by special interests to manage one well.
>
> "I have not advocated the single payer model here," he said, "because our government is too corrupt. Medicare is a large insurance company whose board of directors (Ways and Means and Senate Finance) accept payments from vendors to the company. In the private market, that would get you into trouble."
>
> The key to a single-payer system is that the government sets prices. Usually, it empowers boards of independent experts who set those prices low. Reinhardt's argument is that in the United States, health industry interests have so much sway over Congress that the prices would end up being set by health-care interests.
>
> "When you go to Taiwan or Canada," Reinhardt said, "the kind of lobbying we have here is illegal there. You can't pay money to influence the party the same way. Therefore the bureaucrats who run these systems are pretty much insulated from these pressures. Here you have basically a board of directors in the House Ways and Means Committee that gets money from lobbyists both at the regulatory writing stage and during normal operations. And they can call an administrator and demand they stop something from happening."

Uwe's views on a single payer for the United States remained unchanged. The *New York Times* in its September 18, 2017, *The Upshot*, perhaps best sums up Uwe's views on a single-payer system for the United States:[16]

> Uwe Reinhardt, who has analyzed health care systems around the world for half a century, has been a longtime supporter of single-payer, although he has said he doesn't believe the United States could manage that system well because it's captured by special interests.

On a Canadian-style single-payer Medicare-for-all system for the United States, Uwe wrote this as early as 2007 in an article in the *Milken Institute Review*:[17]

> I don't view the Canadian health care system as a model for the United States for at least two reasons. First, the highly egalitarian precepts inherent in the Canadian approach do not seem compatible with Americans' preference for letting money talk when it comes to health care—or, for that matter, education or the administration of justice. Second, single-payer government-run health systems are especially difficult to administer well in a political system so open to influence through campaign contributions.
> By the same token, though, I don't buy the argument that government-run single-payer health systems are inherently less efficient than market-oriented health systems. In the end, each nation must decide which style of rationing—by the queue or by price and ability to pay—is most compatible with its culture. Mantras about the virtues of markets are no substitute for serious ethical conviction.

On a high performing health care system. Asked by the *Fiscal Times* in an interview, "What would a high-performing national health care system look like?," Uwe said:[18]

> I think the Germans, the Swiss, the Dutch have a perfectly fine approach. It's not a single-payer system. While I'm a Canadian I am not for [single-payer] in the U.S. because we do not have a political system that can handle it responsibly. Canada has a parliamentary system that insulates considerably the public program from lobbying.

In the same interview, Uwe answered the question "So you favor universal coverage but not a single payer system?" as follows:

> For other countries I do [favor single-payer] but we can't run it. You need a responsible system of governance. Whatever you can say about U.S. governance, you cannot call it responsible. You really couldn't. I think the founding fathers gave us an impotent government that acts quite irresponsibly. I don't think parliamentary systems are that bad.

On the idea of a public option—"a public health insurance agency, typically a government-run agency, that can compete with private insurers"[19]—and the impact of a public health insurance plan like a Medicare-for-all on the private insurance industry in the United States. Uwe testified before the House Ways and Means Committee at a congressional hearing on this important topic on April 22, 2009, and had the following exchange with the committee's chairman, Congressman Jim McDermott, who represented Washington State's Seventh District from 1989 to 2017 and was a proponent of a

public option as part of the Affordable Care Act.[20] Congressman McDermott asked:

> In today's hearing let's assume that there is going to be a
> public option. My problem with a public option is how to
> design it so it does not become a dumping ground for the
> problem cases of the insurance industry that they want to
> get rid of.... I would like to ask, if Medicare was made the
> public option, what would be necessary in national insur-
> ance regulation to prevent private companies who want to
> dump their people who are problematic into either the pri-
> vate insurance companies' or the private manufacturers
> into the government plan. What would you have to do to
> make that so it would actually work?

To that Uwe responded:

> Well, most other nations that have only private insurance
> options, or they could have a public one, use a risk-adjustment
> mechanism. Germany quite explicitly does that, so that
> after the enrollment period is over, they assess the risk that
> each plan ended up with and then have compensation pay-
> ments, that is, plans that end up with younger people have
> their people make a payment to this risk fund, and plans
> with sicker people get a payment from that. So if you have
> an insurance market with a public plan and private plans,
> you would use that same mechanism. I think the Germans
> do it, the Dutch do it; the Swiss do it as well. And the risk
> adjusters you need for that are pretty well understood now
> by health services researchers. But that's the most practical
> way to deal with it. So if the public plan actually ended up
> with a sicker risk pool, private plans with a healthier pool
> would have to make a payment so that the risk pool would

be equalized. I actually talk about that in my stated [written testimony]. . . . See, the "playing field" issue is not just payment, it is also the risk pool you end up with. Those are the two things. And the risk pool gets equalized in these other countries by having this compensation mechanism.

Congressman McDermott then asked Uwe:

Is it your view that the creation of a public option like a Medicare-for-all would force people out of the private industry? We've heard this number: 30 percent [of workers] would be forced out of their private plan and into the public plan. Is that your understanding of such a plan?

Uwe responded:

Well, that's the language that gets used. Lewin [a Washington-based health service research firm] doesn't use it, the Lewin Group, but imply it. What that would mean is that many, many employers simply say we will no longer offer employer-based insurance. Of course, those employees then would still have a choice of the public plan and private plans that sell individually-based insurance. So I find that argument specious. I don't think the word "force" is correct English here, because, yes, you wouldn't get it from the employer any more, but, you'd still be able to buy private insurance in the individual market—restructured market. I have never understood this scenario. I don't simply buy the scenario that a public plan would ultimately squish private plans out of existence. And the argument I have heard from . . . —the Galen Institute makes it—that the public plan will then deteriorate and give very low quality care—and they paint the Canadian system. But if there is the option of a private plan, even if they [private plans] had shrunk initially, they would grow again. These people don't seem to understand how markets work, and I am an economist. I cannot believe that if a public plan really didn't play well by the American people, that you wouldn't have immediately a private insurance industry growing out of the ground offering them a better deal. Isn't that how markets work? So somehow there seems to be a lack of faith in the market in this argument.

On changes needed to "better control costs and ensure equitable payment" in the United States. Uwe had long called for an *all-payer* system to replace, over time, the current "price-discriminatory system" we use to pay providers, which lacks price transparency and leads to huge variations in the prices Americans pay for health care. Uwe believed that simplifying the pricing of health care in the private sector should also substantially reduce the administrative cost of health insurance and help lower costs.[21]

Uwe explains what an all-payer system is and what other countries have it where it works well in his November 2011 article in *Health Affairs* on all-payer systems:[22]

> Under an all-payer system, all insurers in a state would pay all providers in a state the same price for a given health service, with adjustments only for differences in the price of the inputs used by health care providers, as under the current Medicare payment systems.
>
> But unlike the current Medicare system, which sets fees unilaterally, the uniform fees under the all-payer system envisaged here would be formally negotiated on a regional basis between representatives of providers and representatives of payers.... The uniform, regional price schedules could also be negotiated in some way by an independent

rate commission with representatives of providers and payers, as is the case in Maryland for hospitals.

Uwe gave examples of all-payer systems that work well:[23]

In developed nations that rely on multiple, competing health insurers—for example, Switzerland and Germany—the prices for health care services and products are subject to uniform price schedules that are either set by government or negotiated on a regional basis between associations of health insurers and associations of providers of health care. In the United States, some states—notably Maryland— have such all-payer systems for hospitals only. Elsewhere in the United States, prices are negotiated between individual payers and providers. This situation has resulted in an opaque system in which payers with market power force weaker payers to cover disproportionate shares of providers' fixed costs—a phenomenon sometimes termed *cost shifting*—or providers simply succeed in charging higher prices when they can.

I might add that Japan is another all-payer system. In Japan, all the providers must abide by the same prices paid by Japan's more than 3,400 insurers based on a single fee schedule for most health care services and products. This all-payer rate setting has allowed Japan to control its health care spending effectively. In 2017, Japan's total health spending was 10.7 percent of its GDP,[24] compared to 18 percent in the United States, despite being the oldest country in the OECD.

Uwe would have been glad to see the five-year extension of Maryland's all-payer system approved in May 2018 (and going beyond hospitals to include primary care physicians and nursing homes effective January 1, 2019),[25] by the Trump administration's CMS through its Innovation Center, an agency created by the Affordable Care Act (Obamacare) to test different payment and delivery models. Since 2014, Maryland's system has generated savings for Medicare that were larger than initially expected. Extension to 2023 of the system is expected to save Medicare an additional $300 million a year over the next five years, according to Maryland governor Larry Hogan.[26]

On price transparency in American health care. For years Uwe wrote about the lack of information (transparency) on prices of health care services and products for patients/consumers, who are urged by their employers and insurers to shop around for cheaper services (presumably of the same quality), as being unfair and inflationary, and berated the insurance industry, providers, and employers for their inaction. Uwe predicted the coming of price transparency in U.S. health care and said this in a December 2013 interview:[27]

> And then finally, people realize there is only so much you can do with utilization control. We're not actually very heavy users of healthcare in America. People started to compare prices. There was the International Federation of Health Plans. They *annually do a survey* of prices and it was quite clear we're paying 2–3 times as much for any health-care service than any other nation.
>
> It's at the point now where I tell providers you can't stop it anymore. I gave a talk recently in New York, called "Barbarians at the Gate." And I said, "You lived in the secure castle with complete price opacity, no one knew what anything cost, which worked really well for you. But you now have these insurgents at the gate, beating at the door, and they're even getting help from inside. Pretty soon you'll be fully transparent."

On overall assessment on health care in America before the Affordable Care Act—the good, the bad, and the ugly. Uwe's views were aired in an extensive interview by the PBS *Frontline* program "Sick around the World," one of the most-watched *Frontline* programs in 2008.[28] Uwe's assessment is as relevant in 2018 as it was a decade ago when the interview was conducted, as the Republican Congress and the courts continue their efforts to undermine key parts of the ACA, which, if successful, could return health care to the pre-ACA days as described by Uwe in the *Frontline* interview:

> Well, if I were to do a balance sheet of the system, the good things are that we have an extremely well-trained labor force, particularly physicians; I don't think any nation trains doctors better. We have the latest technology, simply because we throw so much money [at it]. . . . We are really technology-hungry in this country. That's a good thing.
>
> More and more, our system treats patients like customers, which is actually a good thing; that it's very, in general, customer-friendly—not always, particularly if you're poor, which is a different story, but that is, by and large, a good thing.
>
> And it's very innovative, both in the products we use, in the techniques we use and the organizational structures we use. Those are all very good things, highly competitive.
>
> The bad things are that our financing of health care is really a moral morass. It is a moral morass in the sense that it signals to the doctors and hospitals that human beings have different values depending on their income status. To give you a specific example, in New Jersey, the Medicaid program pays a pediatrician $30 to see a poor child on Medicaid. But the same legislators, through their commercial insurance, pay the same pediatrician $100

to $120 to see their child. . . . How do physicians react to it? If you phone around practices in Princeton, Plainsboro, Hamilton—I did this once, and I think I called 15 practices—none of them would see Medicaid kids.

So here you have a country that often relies on these kids to fight their wars, and yet treats them as if they were lower-value human beings through the payment system. I think that is unique. No other country would make a differentiation like that. So that's a disgrace.

We have 47 million uninsured people at any moment of time, of whom possibly the richest one-third could buy insurance on their own if that market worked, if they could get insurance. But if you're an individual not employed in a large company, and you want to buy insurance and have a pre-existing condition—so you had a skin cancer, say—you won't get insurance, or the premiums will be sky-high. So the market for individual health insurance in America is dysfunctional; it doesn't work, and that is a major problem.

And then, of course, we have, like most nations, the problem of undocumented aliens. In Europe, they just cover them; they just simply cover them. Here, we have this debate in the [legislature]. Every so often comes the edict: Don't give them health care. But you're a doctor or a nurse in an emergency room, and here comes a mother, illegally here, with a child; the child is aching. What are you to do? The legislature tells you, "Don't treat them." . . . That is disgraceful.

On the transformation of the American health care system, and the future of health care in America. Uwe pointed out in a 2013 interview the ongoing transformation of the American health care system toward a two- or multitier system, tiered by income class at point of service; and was, overall, optimistic about health care in America:[29]

> If anything, we would go to a three-tiered system, where it might be that our kids—the ones I teach now—they might say, you don't have to be 100 percent equalitarian in health care. You give everyone a guarantee to something. And so we'll have public clinics and public hospitals, and we'll budget them, and if you're poor, instead of being in Medicaid, you'll go to that hospital. Then for the middle class, you and me, you would have what is called reference pricing. Insurers negotiate prices with different hospitals, and tell their insured, "If you go to this hospital or this hospital and have your baby there, we'll pay 90 percent. If you go to another hospital that is more expensive, you pay the whole difference between this reference price and what they charge you." WellPoint has just introduced that for CalPERS personnel, the state employees in California, only for two procedures—hips and knees—but it lowered the prices by something like 20 percent. And everyone else came down. And then boutique medicine for the elite, which they already have. I personally never begrudge them that. I mean, why should a corporate CEO, when he gets sick, be in a ward when they never mix with humanity as you and I know it? They have their limos, their jets. They have mansions and presidential suites in the Ritz when they go to Washington. It would be almost cruel to say, "When you get sick, we stick you in a ward." I don't mind that they have a little suite—every hospital in America has that. . . . Who cares, as long as they pay for it? It shouldn't be tax funded. I don't think people would begrudge people to

have boutique medicine, other than if it really noticeably affected survival. I mean, if boutique people got the hearts before anyone else in transplant, that would bug people. But if they had butlers, I don't think anyone would care.

I am actually quite optimistic about health care. First of all, it never was that bad a sector. People always say it's the most inefficient sector in the world. It's just all bullshine. If you compare health care to education, health care towers over education in terms of concern about quality, concern about cost effectiveness, et cetera. Compare it to jurisprudence. Have judges ever worried how much time of the jury they pulverize? So I think the health care system actually is a lot better than people claim it to be. We keep beating up on doctors and nurses, and they work very hard. But actually where we should start—there was an Institute of Medicine study out that said we spend $190 billion more per year on administration than we should. It seems to me that should be attacked before I keep hounding more doctors and nurses. There is unnecessary stuff, and people always claim that. But you know I always joke about the vertical and horizontal economists. When we are vertical, we talk a tough game. "Don't do marginally beneficial things." When you are horizontal, even when you are an economist, on an operating table. . . . [Interviewer: You want all of the tests.] Do the low-hanging fruit, the thing that demonstrably couldn't hurt the patients if you went there. One hundred and ninety billion dollars a year would be much more than we need to cover all the uninsured—100 percent universal coverage. So that's what we should go after. For some reason, we talk about evidence-based clinical practice, but not ever about evidence-based administration. What we really need is evidence-based administration. Say, how could you run an insurance system more cheaply than we do? How much should we save? Whatever we are spending, cut it in half. It's achievable with some ingenuity.

On the other hand, there is going to be a lot of innovation coming, made possible for two reasons. One, computational capacity has enormously increased. We now increasingly know how to measure quality. Ten years ago, we really didn't. And the labor market, tragic or not, is sluggish now. In the '90s, the labor market was tight. Employers couldn't do anything. Remember the managed care backlash? Managed care was a good idea. Now, labor is kind of on the run, and it is much easier for employers to impose networks on patients or cost sharing. It's easier to innovate. I go to these venture capitalist meetings. At "Health Datapalooza" [a large annual health care innovations meeting where thousands of health care entrepreneurs share their ideas] these young people dreaming up innovations—IT-based—in claims processing, in wellness—computerized wellness where you have some gizmo that speaks to your iPhone and in your iPhone you get a graph that tells you how your weight's gone this month. Stuff that people need. Make a game out of wellness. There is going to be a lot of innovation coming down the pike. And even within biomedical research, I think you will have a lot of labor-saving innovation. For example, home care that you can do electronically. You don't need a daily visit to these people if the metrics that get radioed to some center look OK.

So I think first of all of the bending of the cost curve, and I am persuaded it's actually more permanent. We always thought it would go up again when the economy improves. I don't think so. It is still very expensive, but more under control than before. And there will be a lot of innovation. I love the kids I teach, I really do. The energy I see there.

When I look at those 30- to 40-year-old entrepreneurs, and they are up at 6, running, making deals, I think they will change things. We are coming into a different era. These people are more open to change. Don't forget, until now, the health system has been a cozy cartel. Everyone knew each other, we're all in this together, and somebody pays the bill. I think those days are over. And you know, it's always been said that necessity is the mother of invention. But for 40 years, invention was the mother of necessity in health care. Somebody invented a machine that went, "beep, beep, beep," rather than just, "beep, beep," and every doctor had to have the "beep, beep, beep" machine. No more. The way device companies and drug companies sell to hospitals isn't any more to the individual doctor and his or her desires, it's to committees. Things are changing. I am actually far more optimistic than I would have been 10 years ago.

A cautionary note on a two- or three-tiered system in America. Such a system inevitably raises concerns about equity for the "bottom tier," by which Uwe meant "uninsured Americans who are poor or near poor—chiefly families of people who work full time at low wages and salaries." As he urged in an interview on PBS in November 2000:"[30]

Let us focus on the bottom tier and say "Let us make it good enough that, as Americans, we could be proud of it." I think that could be done. That would probably be based around managed care. It would have HMOs and it would have gatekeepers in it. You could have all of that if you follow the advice that we should monitor the quality. And it would entitle every American to have at least a right to this basic package and they should pay maybe 10–12 percent of their income towards it, but if they're poor, we should subsidize them. We have to be our brothers' and sisters' keeper. That is the Judeo-Christian ethic. Would this cost an arm and a leg? No. It could all be done for less than a hundred billion additional national health spending a year. It will be less than that, because the uninsured already do get care, they just get the most expensive care too late in the stage of this disease.

Uwe wrote this book principally for the people and policy makers of his adopted country, which he loved. He disagreed with many of America's public policies, but respected the diverse points of views, as he understood they are an essential element of a modern democracy. Uwe only wanted all Americans to have what he believed they deserve—a health care system that will take care of their health care needs with dignity and without bankrupting them or visiting financial hardship on them. He wanted all Americans to have what he had as a little boy in war-torn Germany. I sincerely hope that readers take to heart the many takeaways in the book and become informed participants in the health care debate and efforts at reform to help make America a kinder country, for all Americans and for future generations of Americans.

For international readers, including policy makers in other nations, the key takeaway from the book is to take to heart Uwe's message, which he shared with audiences around the globe:

The U.S. system of *financing* health care is routinely viewed as the bogeyman of health policy—as an example of how *not* to structure a nation's health system.

ACKNOWLEDGMENTS

Tsung-Mei Cheng

This book is an important document on American health care in the first part of the twenty-first century from both an economic and an ethical perspective by one of the most widely respected voices in American health care for more than four decades, whom many regard as a giant in health care policy and economics.

Deep gratitude is due all the individuals and institutions that played important roles, at different times, in making the book possible. As the famous saying "Rome was not built in one day" suggests, no one single individual's achievements come from any one source or origin.

Reflecting on how Uwe became the scholar, the original thinker, and the extraordinary policy expert that he was, Yale comes to mind first and foremost, outside of, of course, Uwe's parents, who gave Uwe his life, good health, and good brains, and helped build his character and humanity. Uwe flourished at Yale. Three professors among many at Yale's economics department stand out in particular to whom Uwe owed a deep debt of gratitude: James Tobin, Richard Ruggles, and William Brainard. The latter two were also Uwe's PhD thesis advisers. They, especially Professor Tobin, inspired Uwe's intellectual odyssey.

Uwe took to heart Tobin's teaching to apply rigorous economic analysis to social issues and Tobin's belief that economics is, or ought to be, an instrument to make society better. That Yale is building a new multimillion-dollar Tobin Center for Economic Policy on its own campus is testament to the man's greatness. Uwe admired Tobin and spoke of him often, especially when frustrated by the too-oft seen faith-based and data-free "policy analyses and recommendations" concerning health care or any other national issue. Uwe's PhD thesis, *Physician Productivity and the Demand for Health Manpower: An Economic Analysis,* which later became a book (1975), as mentioned earlier, was one of the earliest works on health economics and represented "an attempt to bring certain insights gained from economic theory and applied economic research to the task of formulating the nation's health manpower policy during the next several decades." The book launched Uwe's career as a health economist; he always based his policy conclusions and recommendations on rigorous data-driven and evidence-informed health services research and policy analyses.

Uwe also spoke often of his many Princeton colleagues, whom he met in the course of almost fifty years as a faculty member at Princeton—fellow faculty members in the economics department and the Woodrow Wilson School of Public and International Affairs, where Uwe held a joint appointment as the James Madison Professor of Political Economy and Professor of Economics; faculty from Princeton's other schools, departments, and programs; and Nassau Hall—the administration, or "CENTCOM" at Princeton, on whose many committees Uwe had served. Uwe was grateful for their gifts of friendship and the opportunities for invaluable intellectual exchanges which he enjoyed and benefited from greatly. He loved being able to walk into the offices of former and future chairmen of the Federal Reserve, Paul Volcker and Ben Bernanke (both happened to have had their offices next door to Uwe's), to ask them to explain the Fed's latest interest rate hike, or the timing of the next recession, or simply ask Ben questions about the Great Depression, on which Ben is a leading scholar; or into Nobel laureate Sir Arthur Lewis's office to have a discussion on why some nations fail to develop while others flourish; or have endless discussions on pedagogy or corporate finance (Uwe taught corporate finance for years at Princeton) with Burton Malkiel, author of one of the most famous books on stock markets, *A Random Walk down Wall Street*, and a fine teacher (he taught corporate finance before Uwe); or asking another Nobel laureate, Paul Krugman, myriad questions about international trade, on which Paul's work won him the Nobel Prize; or ways to avoid future global financial crises.

I would have liked, on Uwe's behalf, to name and thank all the Princeton colleagues and friends, many of whom work in the administration, buildings and grounds, food services, and so on, whose paths Uwe crossed, for the joy he derived and the things he learned from having known them. Alas, that would be an impossible task, as they are too numerous. Uwe considered himself a lucky man, he often said.

Outside of Princeton, Uwe had many friends and professional peers in both the private and public sectors, including the U.S. and foreign governments, Congress, industry, academia, think tanks, and the media. Uwe also corresponded with myriad members of the public. I know Uwe would like to thank them all too for their friendship, the frank exchanges including the occasional accusation of him as a "socialist propagandist," and what he learned from them.

The book would never have seen the daylight without the strong and enthusiastic endorsement and support of the Princeton University Press. My deep appreciation and gratitude go to all those at the Press who were involved in transforming Uwe's manuscript into the book it is. I thank Christie Henry, director of the Press, and the editorial board for their strong endorsement to publish the book. I thank the editors at the Press, in particular Joe Jackson, senior economics editor, who saw the potential of this book and recommended publication. I am also grateful to Joe for his invaluable editorial suggestions and judgments, and for his guidance in every step involved in turning the manuscript into the book. Other Press team members I would like to thank are Jacqueline Delaney, James Schneider, Maria Lindenfeldar, and Pamela Schnitter for their extensive and dedicated work on various important aspects of the publication process. Their professionalism and expertise in managing the production process of this book are most impressive, and deeply appreciated.

I would like to conclude by thanking Uwe, if I may, and even if it may be unconventional, for finally writing this book to shed light on the highly complex American health care system. Uwe was widely recognized as "*the* person who could explain *anything and everything* about American health care to *anyone*." For Uwe, writing this book, sharing his more than four decades of experiences with and insights into health economics, health policy, and health reforms, was a labor of love and an expression of his gratitude for his adopted country. Last but not least, I thank Uwe also for the opportunity for me, with the help of the Princeton University Press, to bring this important book to the American public.

NOTES

Prologue

1. http://www.nytimes.com/1988/11/14/opinion/essay-watch
   -what-we-do.html
2. http://jamanetwork.com/journals/jama/article-abstract/418809
3. http://www.news965.com/news/local/jimmy-kimmel-tearfully
   -talks-about-his-newborn-son-open-heart-surgery/GYbznGpo
   Mp2NiKESMVNUKN/
4. http://www.news965.com/news/local/jimmy-kimmel-called
   -elitist-creep-editorial-about-his-emotional-monologue/uML
   xys1sU9lx8s9dzIM3TL/
5. Hospitals in Singapore have exactly this structure.
6. http://www.startribune.com/mayo-to-pick-privately-insured
   -patients-amid-medicaid-pressures/416185134/
7. http://www.mankatofreepress.com/news/state_national_news
   /state-questions-whether-mayo-insurance-policy-violates-law
   /article_ff98e030-0ac2-11e7-96d2-ab3f1d6c1865.html
8. https://www.statnews.com/2017/03/17/mayo-insurance-medi
   care-medicaid/
9. http://avalon.law.yale.edu/ancient/hamframe.asp
10. Hammurabi's code also included penalties for medical malpractice,
    which I shall delicately spare the reader.
11. http://jamanetwork.com/journals/jama/fullarticle/2635616
    ?amp;utm_source=JAMALatestIssue&utm_campaign=03-07
    -2017. See also a seminal and eye-opening study of the quality of

U.S. health care by Elizabeth McGlynn et al. in the *New England Journal of Medicine*.

12. http://content.healthaffairs.org/content/25/1/57.abstract

Introduction

1. Uwe E. Reinhardt, "Is There Hope for the Uninsured," *Health Affairs*, W3-376—W3-390 (Abstract, Sep/Oct 03, 267).
2. http://www.pgpf.org/sites/default/files/0059_income-growth -disparity-full.gif, cited at http://www.pnhp.org/news/2001/august /uwe_reinhardt_commen.php
3. Uwe Reinhardt, "Taking Our Gaze away from Bread and Circus Games," *Health Affairs*, 1995. Cited in Physicians for a National Health Program, "Uwe Reinhardt Comments on LeBow and Sullivan," August 16, 2001, http://www.pnhp.org/news/2001/august /uwe_reinhardt_commen.php
4. If macroeconomists wanted to be honest about it, their work has focused primarily on averages or medians, rather than on the actual variances around these measures of central tendency where data on life in an economy actually can be found.
5. Not their opponents, of course, who always present a dire picture of the U.S. economy and promise to do better once they are in the White House and their description of our economy and health system switches 180 degrees.
6. http://www.medpac.gov/docs/default-source/data-book/june -2016-data-book-health-care-spending-and-the-medicare-pro gram.pdf
7. https://www.cms.gov/Research-Statistics-Data-and-Systems /Statistics-Trends-and-Reports/ReportsTrustFunds/Downloads /TR2016.pdf (figure I.1, p. 4).
8. 100*($75,700–$56,000)/$56,000.
9. See, for example, Edward Luce, *The Retreat of Western Liberalism* (Atlantic Monthly Press, 2017). Luce argues that growing income inequality and the erosion of middle-class incomes has eroded the liberal democratic consensus.

10. As someone who served on Congress's Physician Payment Review Commission (PPRC) during the 1980s and 1990s, I recall that we pegged our recommendations to Congress on the fees Medicare should pay physicians to fees in the private health insurance sector. The rule was not to let Medicare fees fall below 68 percent of comparable private sector fees.

11. http://www.kff.org/report-section/medicaid-spending-growth -compared-to-other-payers-issue-brief/

12. The Medicaid program is jointly financed by the federal and state governments on a state-by-state basis. The federal government's share of Medicaid funding for states ranged from 50 percent to 74.63 percent in 2017, with 50 percent being the baseline, or minimum federal contribution. Rates higher than 50 percent are calculated based on the per capita income of the state.

Chapter 1: U.S. Health Spending

1. The OECD excludes from "health spending" certain items included in the health spending data assembled and published by the Centers for Medicare and Medicaid Services (CMS) of the U.S. Department of Health and Human Services. Therefore, the OECD numbers are slightly lower than those published by the CMS, but the relative magnitude of spending among nations is indicative.

2. http://www.kff.org/report-section/health-care-costs-a-primer -2012-report/

3. http://content.healthaffairs.org/content/22/6/27.full.pdf+html

4. https://www.healthaffairs.org/toc/hlthaff/22/3

5. http://content.healthaffairs.org/content/12/3/152.full.pdf

6. https://hbr.org/2013/09/the-downside-of-health-care-job-growth

7. https://www.ahip.org/health-care-dollar/

8. file:///C:/Users/reinhard/AppData/Local/Microsoft/Windows/ INetCache/Content.Outlook/AWOEYNZM/IPS%20July%20 Navigator%202017%20(002).pdf

9. https://newsatjama.jama.com/2017/04/25/jama-forum-where -does-the-health-insurance-premium-dollar-go/

10. http://content.healthaffairs.org/content/30/8/1443.abstract
11. https://www.nytimes.com/2017/03/29/magazine/those-indecipherable-medical-bills-theyre-one-reason-health-care-costs-so-much.html
12. http://www.nejm.org/doi/full/10.1056/NEJMe030091
13. https://www.washingtonpost.com/news/wonk/wp/2017/01/11/trump-on-drug-prices-pharma-companies-are-getting-away-with-murder/?utm_term=.614b12412c86
14. http://www.uhfnyc.org/assets/1574
15. https://www.bloomberg.com/news/articles/2017-04-06/blame-game-over-high-drug-prices-gets-worse-with-lobby-s-new-ad
16. http://healthpolicy.usc.edu/Flow_of_Money_Through_the_Pharmaceutical_Distribution_System.aspx
17. http://www.reuters.com/article/us-pfizer-pricing-idUSKBN18T2QF
18. http://www.modernhealthcare.com/article/20160308/NEWS/160309856
19. http://www.medpac.gov/docs/default-source/reports/chapter-5-medicare-part-b-drug-and-oncology-payment-policy-issues-june-2016-report-.pdf?sfvrsn=0
20. https://economix.blogs.nytimes.com/2009/05/29/the-trouble-with-flexible-spending-accounts/
21. All expenditures that are made out of pretax income or made tax deductible embody a classic tax-and-transfer mechanism. If P is the price buyers pay the vendor for a thing, then under tax-deductibility the net, out-of-pocket price the buyer pays is $P(1-t)$, where t is the marginal income tax rate faced by the buyer. In effect, the buyer receives a public subsidy equal to tP. The higher the buyer's marginal tax rate is, the higher that subsidy will be. To keep its budget balanced, the government then has to recover its lost revenue from other taxpayers. In that sense tax-deductibility is just another tax-and-transfer mechanism. It is why economists accurately describe this form of tax preference a "tax expenditure," on par with other government expenditures.
22. http://healthaffairs.org/blog/2016/10/03/tax-deductibility-as-a-regressive-federal-subsidy/

23. http://money.cnn.com/2017/03/10/news/economy/hsa-republican
    -bill/index.html

24. This is a truly harebrained idea, as it unleashes at year's end an
    inflationary rush to spend down unspent balances in the FSAs. For
    a humorous story on this phenomenon, see https://economix.blogs
    .nytimes.com/2009/05/29/the-trouble-with-flexible-spending
    -accounts/

25. Chad Terhune and Julie Appleby, "Companies offering HSAs
    could bank on big profits under GOP plan." *Kaiser Health News*
    @CNNMoney, March 10, 2017: 6:53 PM ET, https://money.cnn
    .com/2017/03/10/news/economy/hsa-republican-bill/index.html

26. http://www.nytimes.com/2010/11/21/business/economy/21view
    .html

27. David Brooks, "America is Europe." *New York Times*, February 23,
    2012, https://www.nytimes.com/2012/02/24/opinion/brooks-
    america-is-europe.html?_r=1

Chapter 2: Pricing Americans Out

1. "Money income." includes taxes and transfers, but it excludes
   imputed values of publicly financed benefits in kind—e.g., Medicare
   and Medicaid insurance coverage, food stamps, and so on. Although
   these benefits in kind surely have value to their recipients, it is not
   clear what monetary value one should assign to them. After all, the
   money for health benefits in kind granted the poor does not go to
   the poor at all, but instead to the doctors, hospitals, and other providers of health care who produce and deliver those benefits in
   kind to patients. So, for example, if the government raised the fees
   it pays doctors for the services they have rendered the poor and consequently the doctors' incomes went up, would it be reasonable to
   say that the "income" of the poor has risen in like amount?

2. https://www.nytimes.com/2017/06/03/business/economy/high
   -end-medical-care.html?mcubz=1&_r=0

3. http://jamanetwork.com/journals/jama/fullarticle/2565273

4. http://www.npr.org/sections/health-shots/2017/04/10/52300
   5353/how-u-s-health-care-became-big-business

Chapter 3: Facts about Our Health Care System

1. http://news.yale.edu/2015/12/15/hospital-prices-show-mind
   -boggling-variation-across-us-driving-health-care-costs
2. http://www.healthcarepricingproject.org/sites/default/files/pricing
   _variation_manuscript_0.pdf
3. http://content.healthaffairs.org/content/25/1/57.full.pdf+html
4. http://content.time.com/time/subscriber/article/0,33009,
   2136864,00.html
5. https://www.amazon.com/Americas-Bitter-Pill-Politics-Health
   care/dp/0812986687
6. https://www.amazon.com/American-Sickness-Healthcare-Became
   -Business/dp/1594206759
7. https://www.youcaring.com/blog/2016/truth-medical-bankruptcy
8. http://content.healthaffairs.org/content/25/1/57.abstract
9. http://content.healthaffairs.org/content/30/11/2125.full
10. https://www.vox.com/2015/10/14/9528441/high-deductible
    -insurance-kolstad
11. http://www.nber.org/papers/w21632?utm_campaign=ntw&utm
    _medium=email&utm_source=ntw
12. https://www.nytimes.com/2014/09/29/us/costs-can-go-up-fast
    -when-er-is-in-network-but-the-doctors-are-not.html?action
    =click&contentCollection=The%20Upshot&module=Related
    Coverage&region=EndOfArticle&pgtype=article
13. http://catalyst.nejm.org/out-of-network-physicians-emergency
    -billing/
14. https://www.nytimes.com/2014/09/21/us/drive-by-doctoring
    -surprise-medical-bills.html?mcubz=1&_r=0
15. https://www.cfr.org/report/evolving-structure-american-eco
    nomy-and-employment-challenge
16. https://www.wsj.com/articles/how-many-jobs-does-obamacare
    -kill-1499296604
17. http://theincidentaleconomist.com/wordpress/expanded-cove
    rage-has-pushed-health-services-employment-up-by-roughly
    -240000-jobs/

18. http://theincidentaleconomist.com/wordpress/expanded
    -coverage-has-pushed-health-services-employment-up-by-roughly
    -240000-jobs/
19. http://www.commonwealthfund.org/publications/issue-briefs
    /2017/jun/ahca-economic-and-employment-consequences
20. https://www.congress.gov/bill/115th-congress/house-bill/1628
21. https://www.nytimes.com/2017/02/13/upshot/medical-mystery
    -why-is-back-surgery-so-popular-in-casper-wyo.html
22. https://fred.stlouisfed.org/release/tables?rid=53&eid=15274
23. https://stats.oecd.org/Index.aspx?DataSetCode=REV

Chapter 4: Who Actually Pays for Health Care?

1. It is sometimes assumed that single-payer systems imply rationing
   health care. However, imagine what Canada could not offer patients
   if it chose to spend 18 percent of its GDP on health care, as does
   the United States.
2. http://www.cnbc.com/2015/07/16/medicare-medicaid
   -popularity-high-ahead-of-birthday.html
3. https://www.congress.gov/bill/108th-congress/house-bill/1
4. http://jamanetwork.com/journals/jama/fullarticle/2533490
5. I frequently point out to my students that a U.S. Marine Corps pla-
   toon also is a purely socialized enterprise. The marines are government employees, and their equipment is all government owned.
   I point it out lest students have lazy, knee-jerk reactions solely to
   labels, rather than *thinking* about different forms of enterprise.
6. http://content.healthaffairs.org/content/30/9/1630.full.pdf+html
7. To repeat a point made earlier (chapter 1, note 21), all expenditures that are made out of pretax income or made tax deductible
   embody a classic tax-and-transfer mechanism. If P is the price buyers
   pay the vendor for a thing, then under tax-deductibility the net,
   out-of-pocket price the buyer pays is $P(1-t)$, where t is the marginal
   income tax rate faced by the buyer. In effect, the buyer receives a
   public subsidy equal to tP. The higher the buyer's marginal tax rate
   is, the higher that subsidy will be. To keep its budget balanced, the

government then has to recover its lost revenue from other tax-payers. In that sense tax-deductibility is just another tax-and-transfer mechanism. It is why economists accurately describe this form of tax preference a "tax expenditure," on par with other government expenditures.

8. https://www.cbo.gov/budget-options/2013/44903
9. https://www.cbo.gov/publication/51385

Chapter 5: Value for the Money Spent

1. https://www.health-holland.com/public/news/2016/11/health-affairs-rapport-2016.pdf
2. https://kaiserfamilyfoundation.files.wordpress.com/2016/01/8806-the-burden-of-medical-debt-results-from-the-kaiser-family-foundation-new-york-times-medical-bills-survey.pdf
3. http://www.commonwealthfund.org/~/media/files/publications/in-the-literature/2016/nov/1915_osborn_2016_intl_survey_ha_11_16_2016_itl_v2.pdf
4. http://www.nejm.org/doi/full/10.1056/NEJMsb1706645#t=article
5. https://www.ncbi.nlm.nih.gov/books/NBK154484/
6. https://www.cdc.gov/diabetes/data/center/slides.html
7. http://www.healthsystemtracker.org/indicator/health-well-being/life-expectancy
8. http://www.nationalacademies.org/hmd/~/media/Files/Report%20Files/2013/US-Health-International-Perspective/USHealth_Intl_PerspectiveRB.pdf
9. Suppose it is expected that 900,000 of a 1 million cohort of babies born now will survive to age thirty. Then the currently projected age thirty survival probability for this cohort would be 0.9. To calculate life expectancy at birth, one must project these survival probabilities for all ages from one to at least one hundred. It is a daunting guessing game.
10. http://www.sciencedirect.com/science/article/pii/S2049080113700189

11. http://content.healthaffairs.org/content/31/9/2114.full.pdf +html

12. http://www.nationalacademies.org/hmd/~/media/Files/Report %20Files/2013/US-Health-International-Perspective/USHealth _Intl_PerspectiveRB.pdf

13. https://hbr.org/2015/10/how-the-u-s-can-reduce-waste-in-health -care-spending-by-1-trillion

14. https://www.budget.senate.gov/imo/media/doc/davidcutler.pdf

15. http://businessroundtable.org/resources/the-business-roundtable -health-care-value-index-executive-summary

Chapter 6: The Social Role of Health Care

1. http://www.cbc.ca/healthcare/final_report.pdf\

2. By a quirk of history, the German government has always paid half of the civil servants' reasonable medical bills, leaving civil servants to pick up the rest. Therefore, for civil servants, it is cheaper to buy private health insurance for their half of the medical bill than to pay the income-dependent premiums for insurance under the Statutory Health Insurance (SHI) system. Were it not for that quirk in the law, the percentage of Germans covered by private health insurance would be lower than 10 percent.

3. For the most part, people covered by private health insurance enjoy better amenities (somewhat longer physician visits, private rooms in hospitals with more amenities, and treatments by a "Chef Arzt" (department head) who, however, does not necessarily deliver better-quality care than do younger hospital-based physicians.

4. https://www.cbo.gov/system/files/115th-congress-2017-2018 /costestimate/52849-hr1628senate.pdf

5. http://www.kff.org/interactive/premiums-and-tax-credits-under -the-affordable-care-act-vs-the-senate-better-care-reconciliation -act-interactive-maps/?utm_campaign=KFF-2017-June-Senate -BCRA-Tax-Credit-Map&utm_source=hs_email&utm_medium =email&utm_content=53551980&_hsenc=p2ANqtz-9De2pz5jp wbbCQxfVI5fDccb5aWako86Etgg64gxuycDKTYPF7VJuxy

RmjbWjQlaOZ4bjdXEtdRcblmUZ_APD8_uI2Ug&_hsmi
=53551980

Chapter 7: The Mechanics of Commercial Health Insurance

1. The loading factor L could be a percentage markup, as in the equations above, or an additive markup. A percentage markup makes more sense, because insured members with high expected medical spending tend to require more administrative activity on the part of the insurer.
2. https://newsatjama.jama.com/2017/04/25/jama-forum-where -does-the-health-insurance-premium-dollar-go/
3. http://theincidentaleconomist.com/wordpress/where-is-the -outrage-over-employer-sponsored-coverage-in-the-rate-shock -debate/
4. http://www.washingtonexaminer.com/mulvaney-agrees-with -jimmy-kimmel-test/article/2622843
5. https://www.budget.senate.gov/imo/media/doc/SENATE HEALTHCARE.pdf
6. http://content.healthaffairs.org/content/23/4/167.full
7. New Jersey has since changed that by signing a bill into law in May 2018 imposing a mandate on all New Jersey residents to have health insurance or pay a penalty.

Chapter 8: The Elephant in the Room

1. http://www.politico.com/story/2017/02/trump-nobody-knew -that-health-care-could-be-so-complicated-235436

Chapter 9: The Ethical Vision of Obamacare

1. https://www.kff.org/health-reform/fact-sheet/summary-of-the -affordable-care-act/
2. https://www.kff.org/health-reform/fact-sheet/summary-of-the -affordable-care-act/

3. These percentages have increased slightly since 2014, at an annual compound rate of 0.66 percent.

4. http://content.healthaffairs.org/content/29/8/1442.long

5. https://aspe.hhs.gov/system/files/pdf/212721/2017Marketplace LandscapeBrief.pdf

6. http://www.thefiscaltimes.com/2016/11/01/Here-s-How-Much -Obamacare-Premiums-Are-Rising-All-50-States

7. https://aspe.hhs.gov/system/files/pdf/212721/2017Marketplace LandscapeBrief.pdf

8. https://obamacare.net/2017-federal-poverty-line/

9. The Obamacare insurance exchanges offer four types of health plans, which vary by the fraction of the total actuarial cost of the mandated benefit package that is covered by the plan. On average, the Bronze plan covers 60 percent of the actuarial cost, the Silver plan 70 percent, the Gold plan 80 percent, and the Platinum plan 90 percent. The federal subsidies toward the premium are based on the second-cheapest Silver plan in the insured's market area.

10. http://acasignups.net/16/10/04/well-what-do-you-know-hhs -confirms-millions-exchange-enrollees-may-qualify-subsidies

11. We often boast that ours is a "country of laws, not of men." In fact, however, it seems more and more the other way around. What "the law" is at any moment in time seems to depend heavily on whether appeals court and Supreme Court judges are Republicans or Democrats.

Chapter 10: Health Reform Proposals of 2017

1. http://money.cnn.com/2017/05/04/news/economy/obamacare -republican-health-care/index.html
http://www.latimes.com/projects/la-na-pol-obamacare-repeal/

2. http://files.kff.org/attachment/Proposals-to-Replace-the -Affordable-Care-Act-Summary-of-the-American-Health-Care -Act

3. http://healthaffairs.org/blog/2017/06/29/what-makes-covering -maternity-care-different/

4. http://healthblog.ncpa.org/obamacares-war-on-men/#sthash.JGb2idvM.dpbs

5. http://www.rawstory.com/2013/11/fox-news-guest-obamacare-is-a-war-on-bros-because-rates-are-same-as-women/

6. http://www.cnn.com/2017/03/10/politics/shimkus-prenatal-care-comments/index.html

7. https://www.washingtonpost.com/opinions/no-theres-no-war-on-men-in-health-care/2017/03/14/05b8440e-0822-11e7-b77c-0047d15a24e0_story.html?utm_term=.a5461e7194ae

8. Research has shown that the quality of a female fetus's eggs is influenced by the in utero experience of that fetus.

9. http://www.latimes.com/projects/la-na-pol-obamacare-repeal/

10. http://www.kff.org/health-reform/issue-brief/how-affordable-care-act-repeal-and-replace-plans-might-shift-health-insurance-tax-credits/

11. https://www.cbo.gov/system/files/115th-congress-2017-2018/costestimate/hr1628aspassed.pdf

12. http://www.kff.org/health-reform/issue-brief/how-affordable-care-act-repeal-and-replace-plans-might-shift-health-insurance-tax-credits/

13. https://www.forbes.com/sites/theapothecary/2017/03/07/house-gops-obamacare-replacement-will-make-coverage-unaffordable-for-millions-otherwise-its-great/#7172dae037fd

14. https://www.nytimes.com/2017/06/13/us/politics/trump-in-zigzag-calls-house-republicans-health-bill-mean.html?mcubz=1&_r=0

15. https://www.nbcnews.co,/politics/white-house/trump-gop-health-care-bill-will-be-generous-kind-heart-n771626

16. https://www.budget.senate.gov/imo/media/doc/SENATE HEALTHCARE.pdf

17. https://www.nytimes.com/2017/06/22/opinion/senate-health-care-bill.html

18. The expansion was a deal state governors literally had a hard time refusing. Under the provision, the federal government paid 100 percent of the cost of the expansion for the first three years, and 90 percent forever thereafter.

19. https://www.cms.gov/research-statistics-data-and-systems/statistics-trends-and-reports/nationalhealthexpenddata/nationalhealthaccountshistorical.html
20. https://inflationdata.com/Inflation/Consumer_Price_Index/HistoricalCPI.aspx?reloaded=true
21. https://youtube.com/watch?v=Dx1xtKbEtfE
22. U.S. Senate, https://www.budget.senate.gov/bettercare
23. https://www.vox.com/policy-and-politics/2017/6/22/15854790/conservatives-rage-tweeting-senate-health-care-bill-obamacare-lite
24. https://www.healthpocket.com/healthcare-research/infostat/2017 obamacare premiums-deductibles#.WU7hXpDytPZ
25. https://obamacarefacts.com/insurance-exchange/cost-sharing-reduction-subsidies-csr/
26. The Affordable Care Act of 2010 included such a waiver (called Section 2332 waivers), but states had to offer benefit benchmark packages at least as generous as those under regular Obamacare coverage. That requirement has been dropped in the BCRA, so that states can obtain waivers from the secretary of health and human services even if they offer benchmark benefit packages less generous than those on the regular exchanges.
27. https://www.cbo.gov/publication/52849
28. https://www.cbo.gov/system/files/115th-congress-2017-2018/costestimate/52849-hr1628senate.pdf
29. https://www.forbes.com/sites/theapothecary/2017/03/07/house-gops obamacare-replacement-will-make-coverage-unaffordable-for-millions-otherwise-its-great/#6b89dec237fd
30. https://www.washingtonpost.com/opinions/the-senates-health-care-bill-could-be-one-of-the-gops-greatest-accomplishments/2017/06/24/75473678-585d-11e7-ba90-f5875b7d1876_story.html?utm_term=.74f8636aa467
31. https://www.vox.com/policy-and-politics/2017/6/26/15870346/avik-roy-senate-health-care-bill-interview
32. https://www.nytimes.com/2017/06/24/opinion/sunday/republican-health-care-bill.html

33. https://www.nytimes.com/2017/03/28/opinion/can-elephants
-learn-from-failure.html?mcubz=1&_r=0
34. https://www.nytimes.com/2017/07/27/us/politics/obamacare
-partial-repeal-senate-republicans-revolt.html
35. http://money.cnn.com/2017/07/27/news/economy/senate-skinny
-repeal-health-care/index.html

Conclusion

1. http://prospect.org/article/averting-health-care-backlash-0
2. https://economix.blogs.nytimes.com/2012/06/29/health-care
-solidarity-vs-rugged-individualism/?_r=0
3. One could contemplate giving them a tax refund equal to the estimated average annual tax subsidy to the social solidarity pools.

Epilogue

1. Jennifer Greenstein Altmann, "Reinhardt Speaks Frankly as Leading Voice on Health Care," *Princeton Weekly Bulletin*, September 22, 2008, available at https://www.princeton.edu/news/2008/09/25/reinhardt-speaks-frankly-leading-voice-health-care. Accessed January 2, 2019.
2. Christopher L. Eisgruber, "Remembering Uwe Reinhardt," *Princeton Alumni Weekly*, May 16, 2018, available at https://paw.princeton.edu/article/remembering-uwe-reinhardt. Accessed December 31, 2018.
3. Uwe E. Reinhardt, "JAMA Forum: Why Are Private Health Insurers Losing Money on Obamacare?," *Journal of the American Medical Association* (JAMA) Forum, August 25, 2016, available at https://newsatjama.jama.com/2016/08/25/jama-forum-why-are-private-health-insurers-losing-money-on-obamacare/. Accessed January 2, 2019.
4. Altmann, "Reinhardt Speaks Frankly as Leading Voice on Health Care."
5. "The Passing of Uwe Reinhardt: Statement from Drew Altman, President and CEO, Henry J. Kaiser Family Foundation," *Medicare*

Agent News, November 20, 2017, available at http://medicareagent news.blogspot.com/2017/11/the-passing-of-uwe-reinhardt.html. Accessed December 19, 2018.

6. Michael Hotchkiss, "The Next Four Years: Health," Office of Communications, Woodrow Wilson School of Public and International Affairs, Princeton University, September 27, 2016.

7. Ibid.

8. https://www.cms.gov/research-statistics-data-and-systems/ statistics-trends-and-reports/nationalhealthexpenddata/ nhe-fact-sheet.html. Last modified December 6, 2018.

9. Niv Elis, "CBO Downgrades Economic Growth Projection for 2018," *The Hill*, August 13, 2018, available at https://thehill.com /policy/finance/401602-cbo-downgrades-economic-growth -projection-for-2018. Accessed December 29, 2018.

10. Michael Hotchkiss and B. Rose Kelly, "Q&A. What a Trump Presidency Means for the Affordable Care Act," Office of Communications, Woodrow Wilson School of Public and International Affairs, Princeton University, November 16, 2016.

11. Henry J. Kaiser Family Foundation, "Key Facts about the Uninsured Population," available at https://www.kff.org/uninsured /fact-sheet/key-facts-about-the-uninsured-population/. Accessed December 26, 2017.

12. *Washington Journal*, "Uwe Reinhardt on Health Care Costs," aired on C-SPAN, October 13, 2009, available at https://www.c-span.org /video/?289441-7/uwe-reinhardt-health-care-costs&start=4. Accessed January 1, 2019.

13. Hotchkiss and Kelly, "Q&A."

14. "A Conversation with Uwe E. Reinhardt, PhD: Health Care Deserves More Respect," *Managed Care*, November 23, 2013, available at https://www.managedcaremag.com/archives/2013/11 /conversation-uwe-e-reinhardt-phd-health-care-deserves-more -respect. Accessed December 26, 2018.

15. Ezra Klein, "Is the U.S. Too Corrupt for Single-Payer Health Care?," *Washington Post*, January 16, 2014, available at https://www .washingtonpost.com/news/wonk/wp/2014/01/16/is-the-u-s-too

-corrupt-for-single-payer-health-care/?utm_term=.4952fbcdf5b7. Accessed January 10, 2019.

16. Aaron E. Carroll and Austin Frakt, "The Best Health Care System in the World: Which One Would You Pick?," *The Upshot, New York Times*, September 18, 2017, available at https://www.nytimes.com /interactive/2017/09/18/upshot/best-health-care-system-country -bracket.html. Accessed January 1, 2019.

17. Uwe E. Reinhardt, "Keeping Health Care Afloat: The United States versus Canada," *Milken Institute Review*, Second Quarter 2007, available at http://pnhp.org/system/assets/uploads/2011/05 /MILKEN-REVIEW-CANADA-vs-US.pdf. Accessed January 9, 2019.

18. John Greenwald, "Reinhardt: Repeal Health Care, Make GOP Cut Costs," *Fiscal Times*, November 28, 2010, available at http://www .thefiscaltimes.com/Articles/2010/11/28/GOP-Health-Reform -Repeal. Accessed January 27, 2019.

19. "ObamaCare and the Public Option," ObamaCareFacts.com, July 14, 2016; updated January 31, 2017, available at https:// obamacarefacts.com/obamacare-and-the-public-option/. Accessed January 9, 2019.

20. "Uwe Reinhardt Champions Public Health Insurance before Congress," Congressional testimony before the House Ways and Means Committee on the impact of a public health insurance plan, *Healthcare IT News*, July 9, 2012, available at https://www.bing.com/videos /search?q=Uwe+Reinhardt+Health+Care&view=detail&mmscn =vwll&mid=281471DAFA42E12EFE02281471DAFA42E12EFE 02&FORM=VRRTAP. Accessed January 2, 2019.

21. Uwe E. Reinhardt, "The Many Different Prices Paid to Providers and the Flawed Theory of Cost Shifting: Is It Time for a More Rational All-Payer System?," *Health Affairs* 30, no. 11 (November 2011), available at https://www.healthaffairs.org/doi/full/10.1377/hlthaff .2011.0813. Accessed December 30, 2018.

22. Ibid.

23. Ibid.

24. OECD Health Statistics 2018, available at http://www.oecd.org
    /els/health-systems/health-statistics.html. Accessed December 30,
    2018.

25. Tim Curtis, "Maryland Finalizes Expansion of All-Payer System,"
    The Daily Record, May 14, 2018, available at https://thedaily
    record.com/2018/05/14/maryland-finalizes-expansion-of-all
    -payer-system/

26. "Maryland Governor Signs Federal All-Payer Health Contract,"
    U.S. News and World Report, July 9, 2018, available at https://
    www.usnews.com/news/best-states/maryland/articles/2018-07-09/
    maryland-governor-signs-federal-all-payer-health-contract

27. Gabriel Perna, "Uwe Reinhardt: The Year of Hospital Pricing
    Transparency (Part 1)," *Healthcare Informatics*, December 13,
    2013, available at https://www.healthcare-informatics.com/article
    /uwe-reinhardt-year-hospital-pricing-transparency-part-1. Accessed
    January 27, 2019.

28. *Frontline*, "Sick around the World," aired November 10, 2007,
    on PBS, available at https://www.pbs.org/wgbh/pages/frontline
    /sickaroundtheworld/interviews/reinhardt.html. Accessed Decem-
    ber 23, 2018.

29. "A Conversation with Uwe E. Reinhardt, PhD: Health Care Deserves
    More Respect," interview, *Managed Care*, November 23, 2013,
    available at https://www.managedcaremag.com/archives/2013/11
    /conversation-uwe-e-reinhardt-phd-health-care-deserves-more
    -respect. Accessed December 23, 2018.

30. *Frontline*, "Sick around the World."

INDEX

China: demographics of, 21. *See also* Taiwan

citizen engagement, in health care, 142–43

CMS. *See* Centers for Medicare and Medicaid Services

coinsurance, 37, 52, 70, 103, 122, 131, 145

community-rated insurance premiums: ethical perspective on, 85, 91–95, 97–98, *97*; income redistribution via, 45, *46*; under Obamacare, *46*, 86, *92*, 93, 108, 109; reform proposals on, 111, 121–22, 124–25, 135–37

Congress: as administrative overhead driver, 38–40; insurance for, 8, 46; reform proposals of (*see* reform proposals)

Congressional Budget Office (CBO): on real GDP, 5, *6*, 146; reform proposal analysis by, 83, 101, *112*, 113, *114*, 115, *116*, 122, 125–27, *126*, *128–30*, 151

Consumer Price Index for All Urban Consumers (CPI-U): health care cost growth relative to, *8*, 119–20, *120*; Medicaid constraints based on, 7–8, 119–21

Cooper, Zachary, 47

costs of health care. *See* health care costs; prices

CPI-U. *See* Consumer Price Index for All Urban Consumers

Cruz, Ted, 132

Cruz Amendment, 132–33

deductibles, insurance, 52, 70, 103, 122, 131, 145

demographics: health care costs effects of, 17–21, *18–20*; insurance availability based on, 24–25, *25*

Denmark: health care costs in, *2*, *14*, *15*, *17*

diabetes, 71–72, *73*

doctors. *See* health care providers and hospitals

Douthat, Ross, 131

drugs: distribution system, 32–38, *35–36*; income distribution and ability to pay for, 44; prices of, 21, *22*, 32–38, *33–34*, *36*, 145, 150; rebates on, 37

economic perspectives: on commercial health insurance, 85–98; GDP figures (*see* gross domestic product); on health care costs (*see* health care costs; prices); on income distribution (*see* income distribution); on Medicaid and Medicare, 3–9, *5*, *6*, *8*, 66, 175n10, 175n12; per capita figures (*see* per capita figures); on prices (*see* prices)

elderly adults. *See* aging population

employment: growth of health care workforce, 27–28, *28*; health care job creation or depletion, 57–59, *58*; insurance provided via, *25*,

employment (cont.)
25–26, 37, 42, 62, 66–68, 93,
157, 165
ethical perspectives: on commercial
health insurance, 85–98; distributive social ethics, 1, 81–84, 151; on
Obamacare, 102–9; on reform
proposals, 9, 81–84, 95, 99–101,
110–34, 139–67; social good
perspective, 100–101, 102; on social
role of health care, 81–84, *82*

Flack, Roberta, 120
Flexible Spending Accounts (FSAs),
39, 177n24
Frakt, Austin, 60
France: health care costs in, *2, 14, 15,
17*; health care prices in, 50–51;
health status indicators in, *72, 75,
76*; self-rationing of health care in,
71; social health insurance system
in, 93; value for health care
spending in, *71, 72, 75, 76,* 77
FSAs (Flexible Spending Accounts),
39, 177n24

Gaba, Charles, 105
GDP. *See* gross domestic product
Germany: administrative overhead in,
30, 31–32; all-payer system in, 159;
demographics of, *19*; health care
costs in, *2, 14, 15, 17, 19, 30,*
31–32; health care prices in, 50–51,
159; health status indicators in, *75,
76*; private insurance in, 81, 156,

181n2; risk-adjustment mechanisms in, 156; self-rationing of
health care in, *71*; social health
insurance system in, 65, 81, 93,
139–40, 144, 155, 156, 159, 181n2;
social role of health care in, 81;
value for health care spending in,
71, 75, 76, 77
Goethe, Johann Wolfgang von, 139,
143–44
Gorman, Linda, 111
Graham, Lindsey, 101
gross domestic product (GDP):
growth of real, 5, *6*; health care
costs as percentage of, *3,* 13, 14, *14,*
60–61, 146, 159; health care costs
growth exceeding growth of, 146;
Medicare costs as percentage of,
4–5, *6*; per capita, and ability to
pay, 16, *17*; personal income *vs.,* 61

health care: boutique, *25, 45,* 164;
citizen engagement in, 142–43;
costs of (*see* health care costs;
prices); curious facts about U.S.,
47–61; economic perspectives
on (*see* economic perspectives);
ethical perspectives on (*see* ethical
perspectives); income in relation to
(*see* income distribution); insurance
for (*see* insurance); job creation or
depletion, 57–59, *58*; multi-tiered
system, 162–64, 166–67; payers of
(*see* payers); pre-Obamacare status
of, 161–62; providers of (*see* health